TOKYO

By Fosco Maraini
and the Editors of Time-Life Books

Photographs by Harald Sund

THE GREAT CITIES · TIME-LIFE BOOKS · AMSTERDAM

The Author: Fosco Maraini was born in Florence, Italy, in 1912. He went to Japan for the first time in 1938 as an anthropology student and has been back many times since. He is lecturer in Japanese studies at the University of Florence and is the author of several books, among them *Meeting with Japan* and *Japan—Patterns of Continuity.*

The Photographer: Harald Sund was born in Seattle, Washington, in 1943, where he attended the University of Washington. His photographs have appeared in TIME-LIFE Books, LIFE, Modern Photography and various other publications.

EDITOR: Dale Brown
Design Consultant: Louis Klein
Picture Editor: Pamela Marke
Assistant Picture Editor: Anne Angus

Editorial Staff for Tokyo
Text Editor: John Cottrell
Designer: Roy Williams
Staff Writers: Jim Hicks, Deborah Thompson
Picture Researcher: Jasmine Spencer
Text Researchers: Susie Dawson, Vanessa Kramer, Jackie Matthews
Design Assistant: Shirin Patel

Editorial Production for the Series
Art Department: Susan Goldblatt
Editorial Department: Betty H. Weatherley, Julia West
Picture Department: Cathy Doxat-Pratt, Christine Hinze

The captions and text of the picture essays were written by the staff of TIME-LIFE Books.

Valuable assistance was given in the preparation of this volume by TIME-LIFE Books, Tokyo, and TIME-LIFE Correspondent Ann Natanson, Rome.

Published by TIME-LIFE International (Nederland) B.V.
Ottho Heldringstraat 5, Amsterdam 10 18.

Cover: A Japanese character on a neon sign in the Ginza, Tokyo's famed, frenetic entertainment district, electrically conveys one aspect of a city rebuilt since the war. It translates simply to "new".

First end paper: Folded umbrellas of a traditional construction—light bamboo frames covered with lacquered paper—dangle in a row, for the use of priests at a Shinto shrine.

Last end paper: On a kite, hand-painted by one of Tokyo's kite makers, a glowering warrior evokes memories of the city's past as a stronghold of the samurai, Japan's military caste.

TIME
LIFE
BOOKS

THE WORLD'S WILD PLACES
HUMAN BEHAVIOUR
THE ART OF SEWING
THE OLD WEST
THE EMERGENCE OF MAN
LIFE LIBRARY OF PHOTOGRAPHY
TIME-LIFE LIBRARY OF ART
FOODS OF THE WORLD
GREAT AGES OF MAN
LIFE SCIENCE LIBRARY
LIFE NATURE LIBRARY

Contents

I

City of Contrasts

In the quiet garden of a Tokyo museum a child in Western clothes gazes up at a torii, the simple, ritual gateway that marks most shrines devoted to Japan's ancient Shinto faith. The torii, with two stone lanterns near to the city's oldest traditions. But outside this island of peace—beyond the lens of the camera —spreads the sea of steel, glass and pulsating traffic that is modern Tokyo.

I remember that I reached Tokyo for the first time on a bleak winter morning in 1938. The day was grey, the train I arrived on was grey, the city loomed grey beneath the overcast sky. The clothes in which the people of Tokyo scurried through the murk—even the kimono of which I had heard and expected so much—seemed dyed with a sodden, dull neutrality.

But I remember, too, that in that clay-coloured drabness the white gloves of the station masters and train attendants, the white seats on the multitude of rickshaws, the white slip covers inside the taxis had the visual shock of colour itself and seemed somehow to provide the finishing touch to a picture of smooth, restrained professional composure.

It was very strange to eyes like mine, used to the gaiety and colour of southern Europe. Strange, too, was the silence. I had come to Japan by sea—a long journey taking more than a month, broken by frequent landfalls. I still retained in my mind's eye images of Aden, Bombay, Hong Kong, where colour blazed and rioted, and in my ears I could still hear the pandemoniac roar of those tumultuous ports. Tokyo belonged to areas of experience in which I had not yet ventured and I determined—not, I might add, without a considerable amount of humility—to come to grips with it.

Many years later I find myself still coming to grips with it. For each time I return to Tokyo I confront another city, one that is never quite like the Tokyo I knew on the preceding visit. New buildings spring up; attitudes change. Yet whenever I return I find lurking beneath the surface so much that is old, ageless. The real Tokyo, the hidden Tokyo, can be discovered only by someone with the time and patience to ferret it out. I propose to show you that Tokyo. It will not be easy.

Tokyo is the most confusing and elusive of cities. Go in search of a house, a shrine or a temple and you are on an expedition, the outcome of which can never be certain. Tokyo extends over 930 square miles, and has 23 central wards, in which seemingly identical avenues give access to a maze of winding and nameless alleys, marked by an esoteric lexicon of ideographic signs that are beautiful to behold but full of traps even for the initiated. Before we begin to explore modern Tokyo together, let us go back to prewar Tokyo—my first Tokyo.

Beneath the surface of the city I seemed to discern an unease, and one that was, for an Italian like me at that particular time in history, unhappily not as unfamiliar as the lack of noise and colour. I noted none of the Wagnerian heroics of the Germany I had recently visited, none of the operatic flourishes with which Mussolini was conducting himself and my own people through melodrama to disaster. Yet in Japan there was something sinister abroad. I do not like Customs examinations, but in general I do not find them disturbing. At Kobe that morning, after I had debarked from the ship, my body and even its excretions had been microscopically checked over, my political allegiances, my military status carefully inquired into, my belongings combed for—for what? The year before I had taken part in an Italian expedition to Tibet, and as a graduate student in anthropology I was preparing a series of articles on that remote country, helped by a small library of books and journals that I had carried with me into Japan. There was, for example, a volume on Western China by the botanist Kingdon Ward. "Tibet . . . ? Western China . . . ?" asked a stern Customs officer, looking at me with piercing eyes. "Why should *you* be interested in such places?" I had to write down a careful list of all the books I had with me, giving—for *every* item—name of author, title, publisher, dates and so on. The courtesy, smiles, white gloves could not mask the awareness that I was being watched all the time.

I took the boat train from Kobe to Tokyo and in the next few days began to familiarize myself with the city. It struck me as ponderous, gloomy, with occasional patches of brightness and gaiety in the amusement quarters. I don't know why, but the word "Confucian" kept coming to my mind. Had I not learnt from my readings that a Confucian society was run by "rites and music"? And was not Japan guided, in part, by Confucian principles, brought to the country in the 6th Century. True, there was not much evidence of the music (although I was soon to learn how important patriotic anthems, songs, hymns, dirges could be); but rites, oh rites were paramount everywhere—even in my Western-style hotel.

My wife and I and our then two-year-old daughter were staying at the Imperial Hotel in the heart of the city. The hotel bearing that name (the original was torn down in 1967) is today just another enormous, computerized, air-conditioned, 17-storey building, with row upon row of identical rooms. But in those days Frank Lloyd Wright's famous building still stood proudly; it had miraculously survived the great earthquake of 1923 and was looked upon, by Japanese and foreigners alike, as an architectural wonder. The low, carpeted, slightly mysterious and wholly fascinating interior spaces reminded me of a temple—a shrine to modernism, a blend of East and West hinting of ancient Mayan or Cretan buildings. Within, people spoke in low voices.

The Japanese had taken to the Imperial Hotel, drawn by its exoticism and modernity, reassured by its atmosphere of tradition. Here occurred rites and ceremonies of all kinds. They took place under our noses—commemorations, lectures, weddings, graduation parties, anniversaries, all imbued with a formalism new to my eyes. The occasions may have been different, but the actors varied little: there were always elderly gentlemen with bristly white hair, in ill-fitting morning coats with baggy trousers and

Since there is no consistent system of street names in Tokyo, neighbourhood maps, prepared by the local police, record family names (top right) and are displayed at road junctions in each area to help visitors find their way. The little labels over the door (bottom right) include house number, installation marks for gas, water and electricity, and a record of the licences—for dog, radio and television—held by the occupant.

sagging shoulders. Then, there were genteel grey-haired ladies in those kimonos of melancholy hues, clumsy students in their lugubrious black uniforms, and lots of timid, giggling girls. Speeches and multiple deep bows were unending. And only children under seven broke through all conventions and dared to run, jump, play, and make noises.

Outside the hotel, life seemed to consist of more ceremonies, a perpetual round of them. Even the city traffic, at least in the centre, was slow, majestic. On the bus and tram routes running near the Imperial Enclosure in the heart of the city there was a particular place where passengers were invited, with firmness, to stand and bow towards the palace: "Deep reverence everybody please", the conductor would ask.

I had come to Tokyo on a scholarship for Japanese studies and as part of my duties I had to pay courtesy calls on various officials in different cultural institutions. And of those institutions (the officials are largely forgotten), I received an immediate and indelible impression of ponderousness, not unlike the one of the city I was slowly building up. Misleading it may have been, but powerful all the same. The solid and stolid appearance of the many buildings in which I set foot—those concrete stairs with their massive handrails, those solemn, shiny corridors, those carpeted waiting-rooms with leather-covered sofas and armchairs of prodigious size, depth, width—were meant to impress, and they did.

But there was another side to all this and I had my first experience of it when I went to Tokyo station to retrieve some luggage. On the platform was a crowd of male students with banners, streamers and flags of all sorts, sending off a small group of comrades who had been drafted into the army. They were singing, songs like "*Roei no uta*" (The Camp Guards' Song), with which I was going to be all too familiar in the next few years. Most of these were a curious amalgam of martial fervour and melancholy. The leaders of the crowd were beating time with their hands and nodding their heads. Many of the boys seemed rapt, in a sort of trance, shouting out the desperately long notes of the song with all the force of their lungs, their mouths wide open in ugly grimaces, their eyes half closed, their heads thrown back. Their faces became suffused with passion, the veins in their necks stood out in relief, swollen to near bursting. At the end of the song they screamed a volley of harsh and guttural cheers, and lifted both hands to the shout of "*Banzai*" (Hurrah for the Emperor!). It was all very frightening. I had never witnessed such a collective surrender to emotions so intensely visceral.

Yet outside the station, the enigmatic city was as composed, as silent and well behaved as ever. Had I suddenly gained some new insight into it? In the days ahead I sensed more and more that somewhere beneath the sober surface an inner furnace burned, sometimes with a splendid, sometimes with a sinister flame. Suppressed fury? Or repressed vitality? I could not make up my mind. I began to feel that there might be much more to Tokyo than met my naïve foreign eye.

I went about exploring the city. I soon realized that it was not one city, but a whole collection of cities, towns, villages. It is still that today. There are little alleys of low, wooden houses with fenced-in gardens a stone's throw from the American Embassy or less than half a mile from the Imperial Palace, all in the heart of town. Some of these unmetropolitan districts have an extraordinary charm. Wandering down their narrow streets you suddenly come upon the grounds of a small shrine of the Shinto faith, Japan's indigenous religion, with a diminutive torii, or gate, in front of which children, gaily shouting, play marbles. Or you may chance upon a small shop that sells practically everything—like the proverbial general store in any out-of-the-way little village or on a remote island.

My understanding of the city deepened further when I began to follow up the letters of introduction I had brought with me. I had been told that the Japanese never entertain at home. But, possibly because I enjoyed the advantages of being a young Western student on a scholarship granted by the Japanese Government, I found my wife and myself being cordially received in a number of different Tokyo homes, and by a lucky chance the introductions covered a large part of the spectrum of Japanese society.

One family belonged to that highly Westernized section of the upper classes from which many diplomats and civil servants have come since the reign of the Emperor Meiji (1868-1912). Their house was an amiably mock Tudor mansion. Others were academics with a middle-class background and although their homes were entirely Japanese in style, there seemed always to be an added Western style drawing-room-cum-library, displaying prominently on its shelves a bust of Beethoven, or a small,

Near enough to be heard in a normal voice, a teacher (far right) nevertheless yields to the national love of gadgets and uses a megaphone to direct uniformed secondary school students in front of the main entrance of the Imperial Palace. Willow, bridge and a historic watchtower combine to make this a favourite background for group photographs.

marble Leaning Tower of Pisa, or an image of Abraham Lincoln—all the proper souvenirs of a Grand Tour of the fabled West.

And then there were the Bambas—he a painter, she a poet—a childless couple who have remained my friends. Both diminutive in size, both incredibly gentle and incredibly resilient. When I first knew them, they lived in a wooden hut, hardly larger than a bird's nest, surrounded by a lawn and some trees, in one of those village-like districts of "rural Tokyo". Their tiny home and their toy garden were a natural meeting place for artists, writers, poets, scientists and explorers; the warmth and indefatigable zest for life of the Bambas attracted Japanese and foreigners alike.

Thanks to new friends and acquaintances like these, Tokyo very soon became for me no longer a mere place, a name on the map; it began to acquire an identity, a character defined—as the character of any great city always is—by the way its people conduct their daily lives. Apart from the obvious contrast between the comfort and abundance enjoyed by the upper classes in Italy and the spartan simplicity prevailing in the homes of their counterparts in Japan, the most striking difference for me was in the almost religious quality of public and official life. I had had a hint of it, certainly, in all those offices I visited. But it was to be most vividly confirmed on the day I saw the Emperor.

Preparations of extraordinary thoroughness had begun days before; policemen came round and inspected passports and permits of residence, made inquiries about everybody and gave all sorts of detailed instructions. It was strictly forbidden, for instance, to remain on the upper floors of

Tokyo at nightfall seems to stretch to the horizon, its 930 square miles of brilliant glitter challenging the last gleams of day. The radio and television mast of the Tokyo Tower—59 feet higher than the Eiffel Tower on which it was modelled—lends to the panorama a Parisian look belied by the city's uniformly modern buildings and light-streaked freeways.

buildings along the route of the Imperial progress: "Nobody must look down on the Sovereign!" So, when at last the moment arrived, crowds of people in their best clothes stood in a long row on the pavement.

First came the motor cycles and then motor cars—of a strange, dull magenta colour—crested with stylized gold chrysanthemums, the imperial emblem; and after them, more cars, and more still. But at last the command was given for a deep obeisance. The whole crowd bent forward at such an angle that eyes must have seen only the tips of shoes and *geta*, or wooden clogs. Nobody dared look directly at the sacred person of the *Tenno*, the Emperor. Some of the more intensely patriotic citizens even knelt on the kerb and abased themselves, foreheads to the ground. Impious foreigner that I was, I managed to get a sideways look at the sacred vehicle with its divine-human passenger—and fixed that scene in my mind. It was indeed impressive—not so much because of the person of the Emperor but because of the crowd's response to him.

The air of sacerdotal piety I felt that day pervaded the whole of public life. In the absence of an authentic Japanese church, people seemed to project feelings of religious awe into their officials, both civil and military, and even on to the buildings sanctified by the offices they inhabited. A ministry, an important government office, even a school, could quickly acquire the aura of a shrine or temple. People who themselves were not initiated into the higher mysteries moved about in such places with awe and trepidation far beyond the limits of mere secular respect.

And then came the war.

On December 8, 1941, the morning paper announced the news in a colossal headline, below which ran the Imperial sanction for so momentous a declaration: "We, by the grace of Heaven, Emperor of Japan, seated on the Throne of a line unbroken for ages eternal;" and so on, reminding the faithful of the divinity of their leader and of the ideal of "the Eight Corners of the World under one Roof" (the one roof being the Emperor's rule).

"What a terrible thing!" exclaimed one friend who came to visit me. But soon, as victory followed easy victory and territorial gains became more and more impressive, for most Japanese it ceased to seem such a "terrible thing". They rallied. But the day came when army and navy units had been stretched over too enormous an area of the Pacific and of East Asia, and a slow and inexorable retreat was forced upon them by the Allies. The personal destinies of my little family, tied as they were to events taking place at the other end of the world, in Italy and the rest of Europe, dictated that we would see what happened to Tokyo in the end. We refused to acknowledge Mussolini as the lawful ruler of Italy after the division of the country (between the Allies and the Germans) in 1943 and we were consequently interned at the city of Nagoya, 160 miles west of Tokyo. There, as civilian internees, we passed two miserable years of starvation and humiliation. But this is not the place to write about our experiences at Nagoya. We had

After the saturation air raids of 1945, only a few shells of concrete buildings remain standing in the Sumida River area of central Tokyo. Most of the damage was done by fire storms that raged unchecked through the congested city, totally destroying huge areas and killing more than 100,000 people.

our terrors, and saw and heard and smelt such things as can never be forgotten. On August 14, 1945, the war ended. Immediately after the Emperor's message to his people on August 15, we were turned out to freedom, still stunned by all we had been through, but intoxicated by our release.

What had happened in Tokyo needs to be told, if only because the tragedies of Hiroshima and Nagasaki have, for obvious reasons, so overshadowed it. The raid of the night of March 9-10, 1945, destroyed much of Tokyo with a completeness and thoroughness that would be unbelievable, incomprehensible, had not the two "atomic" cities, bombed on August 6 and August 9 and so much photographed and written about, made such a destruction all too horribly believable. Vast and all-consuming firestorms devoured the wooden buildings that jammed the city; only a few concrete buildings survived. Whirlwinds of flame—*tatsumaki*, the "dragon twists" of the medieval scroll-painters—lashed and writhed over a shattered population, prepared for their onslaught with no more than a row of water buckets. Many thousands of people simply suffocated, gasping for the oxygen so greedily swallowed by the flames; thousands more baked to death, carbonized, in buildings that had seemed to offer shelter but had become roaring ovens; and still more thousands drowned in the crush of those who fled to the Sumida River as a last refuge. In a night, 250,000 buildings had been destroyed and almost 100,000 people—as many as the Imperial armed forces had lost during all the 40 months of the war—had been obliterated.

My wife, daughters and I saw the aftermath of that holocaust some months later. In early September, at the time of our release from Nagoya, we did not know what had happened to Tokyo back in March, and before our train was due to reach the terminus we began as in former years to look for the first signs of the capital. But there were no signs. There was no Tokyo. Under a perfect blue sky an absurd and terrifying desert of rubble stretched for miles in every direction. A few concrete buildings, empty and burnt out, stood here and there like bones. Among the broken bricks and tiles that littered that vast and empty landscape, fragments of melted glass glittered green in the sun. Here and there the charcoaled remains of a tree stood grotesquely alone. Odd incombustible objects survived—mysterious "villages", never observable when Tokyo was there. These were the whitewashed storerooms of stone known as *kura*, each about the size of a log cabin, that had been built next to homes and businesses and in which people kept their valuables. Smaller safes of steel, contorted but intact, marked places where shops, inns, businesses had once thrived.

And yet, as we were to discover, here and there in the nightmare moonscape of destruction there were signs of returning life. Makeshift huts built of half-burnt planks, already covered by the brilliant green leaves of *satsuma imo* (sweet potato) vines, stood along streets where the rubble had been cleared away. Already there were people in numbers enough to be

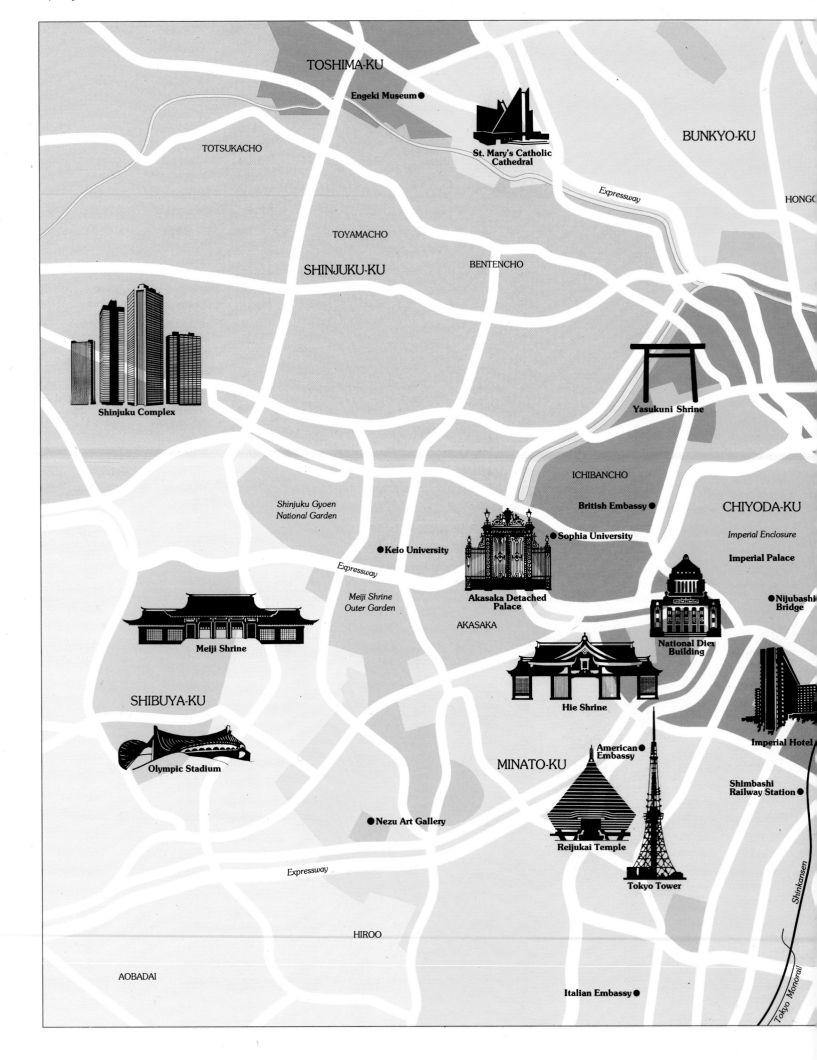

TOSHIMA-KU

Engeki Museum ●

BUNKYO-KU

TOTSUKACHO

St. Mary's Catholic
Cathedral

Expressway

HONGO

TOYAMACHO

SHINJUKU-KU

BENTENCHO

Yasukuni Shrine

Shinjuku Complex

ICHIBANCHO

Shinjuku Gyoen
National Garden

British Embassy ●

CHIYODA-KU

Imperial Enclosure

● Keio University

● Sophia University

Imperial Palace

Expressway

Meiji Shrine
Outer Garden

Akasaka Detached
Palace

● Nijubashi
Bridge

Meiji Shrine

AKASAKA

National Diet
Building

SHIBUYA-KU

Hie Shrine

Olympic Stadium

American
Embassy ●

Imperial Hotel

MINATO-KU

Shimbashi
Railway Station ●

● Nezu Art Gallery

Reijukai Temple

Tokyo Tower

Expressway

HIROO

AOBADAI

Italian Embassy ●

Shinkansen

Tokyo Monorail

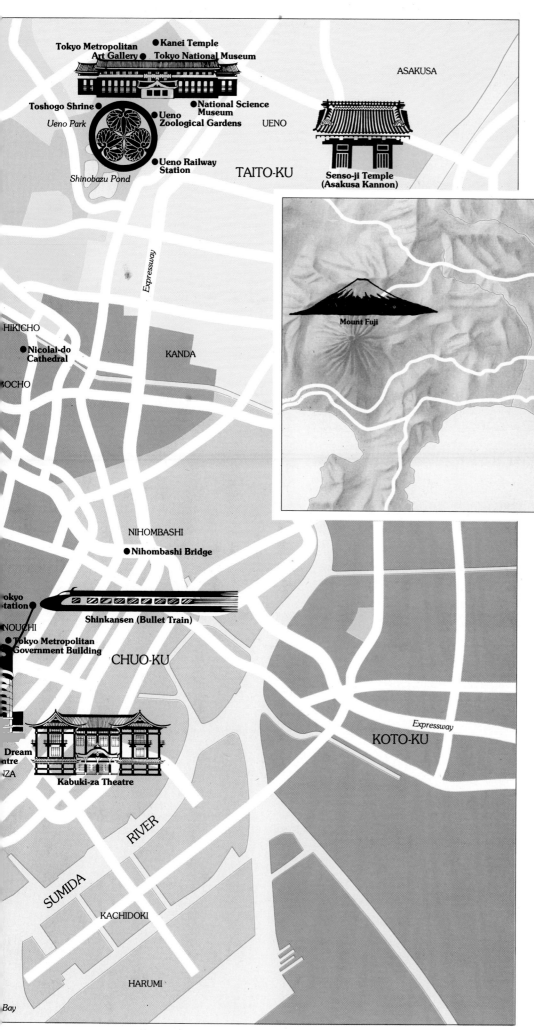

Tokyo Metropolitan
Art Gallery ● ● Kanei Temple
● Tokyo National Museum

ASAKUSA

Toshogo Shrine ● ● National Science
Museum

Ueno Park ● Ueno
Zoological Gardens UENO

● Ueno Railway
Station

Shinobazu Pond TAITO-KU

Senso-ji Temple
(Asakusa Kannon)

HIKICHO

● Nicolai-do
Cathedral

KANDA

Fussa ● Tobu-Nerima ● 930 square miles

Mount Fuji Sumida River

7 Miles

● Chiba

Kawasaki ● ● Tokyo
International Airport

Yamato ● Tokyo Bay

● Yokohama

● Kamakura

NIHOMBASHI

● Nihombashi Bridge

Tokyo
Station ●

Shinkansen (Bullet Train)

NOUCHI

● Tokyo Metropolitan
Government Building

CHUO-KU

Expressway

KOTO-KU

Dream
entre

NZA

Kabuki-za Theatre

RIVER

SUMIDA

KACHIDOKI

HARUMI

Bay

Imperial Super-City

Shown on the map at left is the central core of Tokyo's sprawling conurbation, with its parks, museums, shrines and temples, its shopping and amusement districts, its ultramodern expressways and well-established railways. The city is organized in 23 *ku* (wards), subdivided into *cho* (neighbourhoods), many with their own local character. The imperial capital of Japan only since 1868, Tokyo was a mere village until the 15th Century; its importance dates from 1590, when it became the seat of a powerful military dynasty. Repeated fires and earthquakes (and most devastatingly the air raids of 1945) have caused Tokyo to be completely rebuilt several times. But although few of its buildings predate the Second World War, much of the city's original shape remains: the modern Imperial Palace stands in parkland on the site of the feudal castle, and the surrounding pattern of roads reflects the castle's concentric defences.

The inset map above indicates the city's present vast size—930 square miles—and shows its position on gentle slopes at the mouth of the Sumida River, which flows into the natural harbour of Tokyo Bay. Sixty miles away to the west stands Mount Fuji.

called crowds—mostly still stunned, aimless, helpless, but alive. There was even a kind of commerce along the streets: things were for sale—pathetic little heaps of food, bits of cloth, an old hammer, a few nails. At one corner a rather well-dressed middle-aged woman, her face hidden by a scarf, offered what looked like family heirlooms—a lacquer box, a porcelain vase, a small bronze Buddha. There was all the appearance, but none of the relaxed nonchalance, of the village markets I had seen in the Himalayas a few years before. Here the atmosphere was desperate.

People were not only lost in misery, but seemed to have lost all resilience. Men with lean, hungry faces—some with ugly scars, others with dirty bandages—limped along in a hopeless daze. Women were mostly old, or had made themselves deliberately ugly; the Japanese had been told, by radio and newspapers alike, that the "barbarians from the West" were arriving to plunder, and especially to rape, and that the best defence was, naturally, to be as unattractive and unprovocative as possible. Sullen despair and deep fear seemed to affect even the children, few of whom could be seen playing in the ruins.

If the material destruction was frightening, the inner humiliation, the spiritual shock of defeat was even worse. Rome has fallen so many times —from Alaric to Charles the Fifth and beyond—that its citizens are not utterly cast down when another defeat and a new occupation occurs. Paris and Berlin, too, have known what the losing end of a war feels like. In Tokyo it was unknown, terrifying; most people really had believed in a vague way that the ordinary laws of humanity did not apply to the privileged inhabitants of the "Eight Myriad Islands"; that the August Virtue of the Emperor and his ancestors, in particular of Amaterasu, the sun deity, would confer some sort of mystical immunity from defeat, and a destiny of unique glory. Had not the *kamikaze* (divine wind) sent Kublai Khan's fleet to the bottom of the sea, off Kyushu, in the 13th Century? The same would doubtless happen again.

But it did not. The Emperor, putting an end to the war, had spoken of "enduring the unendurable", and that was exactly how it felt to the Japanese. Hundreds of them, from generals to common workers, killed themselves. The living, however, required a total reassessment of values, an agonizing inner reconstruction. The meaning of everything—man, earth, State, gods, history—had to be reconsidered in the light of the absurd, incredible fact of defeat. The year 1945 was, therefore, not just another date in Japanese history, it was the end and beginning of all things.

Tokyo in September, 1945 was miserable, dirty, feckless. And it had its symbol in the Ueno station. This vast sprawling complex of buildings— with its concrete caves and underground passages, its stairs, corridors and halls—although partly damaged by the bombings functioned as a sort of trogloditic city in its own right, inhabited by desperados, vagrants, prostitutes, orphans. Those who saw Kurosawa's famous 1950 film *Rashomon*

A time exposure turns heavy night-time traffic on an urban motorway into rivers of light snaking between the high-rise office buildings. The city's expressways, an ambitious system begun in the 1960s, have been forced to take devious routes through central Tokyo—sometimes rising three storeys high on pillars, sometimes diving through deep underpasses.

can remember the ruined city gate of Kyoto as a haven for roving monks and bandits. In 1945, Tokyo's Ueno station was a similar haven, in concrete and steel, with campfires and dank corners stinking of urine; it was a dangerous place for all after sunset, for the weak at any time.

Many cities in Europe suffered similarly, but if Tokyo had been unaccustomed to defeat, it was nonetheless a city that had experienced disaster, not once but a number of times. Many of those who witnessed and suffered the holocaust of the great raid still remembered the disaster of 1923, when a severe earthquake was followed by raging fires of a ferocity equal to those of 1945. Then, 60,000 people had died, 35,000 of them together in a single open space near the river.

Fire and earthquake and flood have destroyed the city, wholly or partially, on at least six major occasions in its short 400-year history and have damaged it substantially in hundreds of "minor" incidents over the centuries. In 1657 it was fire, in 1703 an earthquake, in 1772 fire. The Tokyo of today is possibly the fourth or fifth entirely new edition of the city. Each time, as soon as the embers cooled, the tremors ceased, the waters subsided, Tokyo built itself up again. But even that resilience, so aptly encapsulated in the proverb, "Fall seven times but on the eighth get up", might not have been enough to save the city after 1945, had the character of the Occupation been different.

As the Allies moved into Marunouchi, the only part of the city that, because of its concrete construction, had remained more or less intact, the apprehensive citizens realized that they were not to be subjected to something worse than what they had already suffered. Far from being the savages described by the militarists, the enemy behaved with exemplary fairness and restraint. Hope replaced despair, reconstruction began.

The city changed face quickly. Rubble was cleared away. Temporary buildings sprang up. And there was a sudden flowering of amusement quarters with gay colours and lights. Girls of all ages, classes and conditions, seeing that the "barbarians from the West" were not raping them after all, let themselves be raped, one might say, for a small consideration, or out of sheer gratitude, in the general mood of relaxation that followed the terrible years of war. In a curious metaphorical way the cryptic feminine component of the Japanese personality was taking delight in a sort of national "rape" by the great, good, loving, just, stern, sage, strong, blue-eyed shogun—General Douglas MacArthur.

Through a lucky set of circumstances the man and the country were somehow made for each other. General MacArthur "dealt with the Japanese people as an educator", one Japanese has written, "rather than as a Commander of Occupation Forces or as an avenger. The Japanese became his devoted followers." I recall seeing crowds of Japanese, hundreds of them waiting at midday for the moment when the general left his headquarters in the Dai Ichi Seimei building to go to lunch. Even a glimpse of the great man was enough. He was tall and spectacularly democratic as he walked out in shirtsleeves with a couple of unarmed guards, and crossed the road to his Jeep while people spontaneously clapped.

I must say, the first time I saw this happen I was shocked—and a little disgusted. Everything that had been said, written, sung and proclaimed by the Japanese during those years before, had it been all farce and mummery? Or was this now a farce? Mine were the natural reactions of a Westerner brought up in a dualist and intellectualist culture, where things are or they are not, where contradictions are reckoned as unsurpassable barriers, where opposites cannot easily be blended. Slowly I came to understand that what I at first despised, because it seemed so hypocritical, was a text-book case of Japanese pragmatism in action, and not contemptible at all. Japanese pragmatism runs much deeper than its Western counterpart; it implies a kind of union with the secret and sacred forces of life. Facts had proved the *gunbatsu*, the military, to be wrong, and the Allies to be right. It was not opportunism—of which, no doubt, there was a fair share—that made people accept the new regime so willingly, with such incredible enthusiasm; it was, rather, a deep and sincere respect for the inevitability of change.

It took me a while to get used to this new Tokyo—so inconceivably different, both in appearance and in mood, from the one I had known before. But at last I felt confident enough to search for old friends—as I have indicated no easy matter, even at the best of times. Searching for a particular place in a city that had been levelled was like following a mirage. Trams and buses were few. I had to walk most of the way. But at last, with luck, I managed to locate at least a couple of my friends of former days. Some things do not change and fortunately my friends had not.

As much as the city itself, my friends—life-loving people like the Bambas—keep drawing me back to Tokyo. Through them, in part, I have come to know postwar Tokyo; and through them, in large measure, I shall introduce you to the city. There are many ways to enter it, but the most exciting, I think, is from the airport, on a rainy evening. Neon lights of all imaginable colours—most of them nervously jumping, moving, whirling—shimmer in pools or on wet surfaces. And as the taxi speeds towards the centre of town, the highway becomes a toboggan course in which irregular turns follow one another, with sudden dips and climbs. Cars and lorries from the opposite direction rush by like roaring, charging bulls.

On and on the car speeds; we are led on a sort of slalom course by the ribbon of asphalt, which plunges through sudden tunnels, then soars above mazes of bridges, crashes through a forest of towers. Ideograms explode as we pass: Ginza, Kiyobashi, Kanda . . . the names of famous districts. Up we go suddenly on the elevated road and some of Tokyo's great avenues, choked with the metal flow of cars, rotate beneath us like vineyards seen from a speeding train.

Tokyo is a fantastic space-city straight out of H. G. Wells' "The Shape of Things to Come"—a vortex of frenetic human activity, criss-crossed like a giant spider's web by nearly 60 miles of elevated expressways, and encircled by railways and highways, with every inch of space within its compass put to some practical use. Buildings rise higher and higher and spread out even into Tokyo Bay (a plan by the great modern architect Kenzo Tange envisages a whole new city built on a platform over the bay). In the bowels of the earth, enormous, air-conditioned subterranean "cities" take shape. And everywhere are people—people coming, going, climbing, sitting, working, playing; being disgorged through gates, from trains, from buses. According to the official statistics, the city's 23 wards include some nine million inhabitants. But Tokyo is really so much bigger. In its wild growth, it is swallowing up the countryside, and now at least another four or five million people live within commuting distance of its main commercial, business, administrative and recreational centres.

Understandably Tokyo is not a city to speak of in terms of beauty—at least in any conventional terms. But it has a magic all its own. It takes you by the neck, shakes you, turns you inside out and then only slowly does it reveal its heart.

Problems of Pollution and Population

People waiting to cross a street, some covering noses with handkerchiefs, grimace at the sting of sulphurous smog so powerful that it can corrode metal.

Eye-searing air pollution is only one of the afflictions that often make Greater Tokyo's 11 million people feel they live in a bad dream. Ills common to big cities—noise, traffic, public transport problems—escalate to appalling dimensions in this swollen megalopolis. The root cause is too many people in too little space, straining all services to the limit. Housing programmes struggle to keep pace with the growing population. There are relatively few parks, and land has become too costly to create more. Tokyo also has special worries not shared by most other cities. Frequent tremors are reminders of its vulnerability to earthquakes. In addition, parts of it are sinking rapidly as fresh water is pumped up for industrial use, and reclaimed land settles. As a result, a big typhoon—always a threat—could flood much of the city.

This grid system lets pedestrians cross in all directions while traffic waits, an idea borrowed from the U.S.

A Constant Search for Cures

Tokyo keeps testing new palliatives for its ills. Sixty miles of new motorway added over 11 years failed to relieve congestion noticeably; then, as private cars reached the one million mark and accidents mounted steeply, the city tried the opposite approach: closing some main streets to traffic. Authorities are also trying new paving materials to cut vibration damage from traffic, and new road-crossing schemes like the one above.

In a rare, jam-free moment, cars flash over a crossing. Congestion in rush-hours keeps speeds on Tokyo's streets down to 11 m.p.h.—about as fast as a bicycle.

High-Density Pressures

Crowded Tokyo subjects its citizens to stress in
many forms, not least in the sheer competition
for elbow room. With few parks, people spend
time strolling the main streets such as the famed
Ginza. But even on Sundays, when it is closed
to cars, walking along the Ginza calls for more
bumping, halting and agile side-stepping than
most Westerners would consider compatible
with truly pleasant relaxation.

On the Ginza, establishments are almost as closely packed as people. More than 1,100 bars and 500 restaurants are crammed into one-eighth of a square mile.

Passengers await a "hip-pusher" who will pack them in before doors close.

Hell on Wheels for Commuters

Commuters refer to Tokyo rush-hours, when tube and railway
carriages are jammed to 250 per cent of normal capacity, as
"Transportation Hell". Passengers are warned not to board
with their arms in awkward positions lest they get broken.
Babies have been suffocated in the crush. Windows sometimes
shatter and every day dozens of riders lose their shoes.

Commuters race for rush-hour trains in Koenji Station, one of Tokyo's 20-odd terminals. Railways carry over seven million people daily in and out of the city.

The Crush at Poolside

Although Tokyo has more than 70 State and
municipal swimming pools, as well as a number
of privately owned ones that are open to the
public, most of them are crowded to capacity
throughout the hot, humid summer. All charge
entrance fees, and prices at privately owned
pools can be high—yet during the warmest
hours of the day scenes of poolside congestion
like that at right are commonplace.

In sweltering temperatures, lunch-time bathers swarm around the pools at one of Tokyo's swimming centres, competing for space in the teeming water.

2

The Ancient Roots

Just five short centuries ago nothing more than farming villages, fishing hamlets and a small castle marked the Tokyo area, known then as Edo ("The River's Mouth") for the Sumida River that emptied into what is today called Tokyo Bay. But for so relatively young a city, Tokyo has roots that run deep into Japan's past, deep into the soil of Japan.

I am fascinated by origins, and I always wonder when I contemplate a great city what the landscape could have been like before it was trampled and mauled by man into something completely different. I like to think, for instance, of the granite rocks of Manhattan as they once were: crags on a deserted and windswept coast, or of the little island in the Seine, which is the heart of Paris, as a point of minor interest in a luscious, unsullied riverine landscape.

In Rome, I find it easy to cast my mind back; after more than 25 centuries of solid urban existence, the city of cities is still fundamentally "pastoral". Kid and lamb, *caciotta* and *mozzarella* cheese, the produce of pastures and the shepherd's toil are its most genuine and typical delicacies; and sometimes, in unexpected ways, it can still show you more direct evidence of its bucolic past. I shall never forget returning home one very late night in Rome, during the 1950s, and finding the Piazza del Popolo filled with jostling sheep, a turbulent white sea of woolly backs; there must have been 15 or 20 thousand of them, being led through the city on their seasonal migration from the high Abruzzi to the Maremma Plains.

But what changeless past peeps from its hiding-place in changed Tokyo? My conversations with the Bambas, my friends of old, revert often to this theme, for they have an unusually deep historical knowledge of their city. I love to listen as they talk about what they have seen, heard from oldtimers, read, discovered. On the surface, Tokyo looks modern, a spaceship projected towards the future, without a trace of the past, at least as far as there is any visible, tangible evidence of it. Here there is no Tokyo Forum to remind us of the Caesars, no Tower of Tokyo in which the very stones speak to us of past kings and queens. But if you have a friend as knowledgeable and enthusiastic as Hisako Bamba to stop you and say; "Listen! The voices of the past are all around you," you can hear them.

Where the city now spreads, rice was once cultivated and shrines dedicated to gods of fertility and abundance stood among groves of trees. Rice was not only food for the farmers and fishermen, but something wonderful, mystical, sacred. The popular rice-god Inari, had, and still has, mysterious foxes for his messengers. You can see statues of these foxes in Tokyo

In the Imperial Enclosure's East Garden, gnarled tree-roots reach over the mossy stones of an ancient wall, once part of the great Edo castle that stood here. Built originally in 1456, the castle was the seat of the Tokugawa shoguns—military rulers—from 1590 until 1868, when the Emperor took it over. Much restored over the years, it was destroyed in 1945 by wartime fire and a new residence was built for the Imperial Family.

today in front of the shrines devoted to Inari—white, grinning animals with bushy tails. Now the shrines are largely kept up by merchants and businessmen. Although rice remains a Japanese staple, its veneration has declined. Yet the main idea of the Inari cult—prayers for abundance and riches—survives, indeed flourishes, in modern Tokyo.

The first of the several Tokyos I would like to show you is that archaic city of rice and prayers. And the way I will do so is through two *matsuri*, or Shinto festivals. Some 260 *matsuri* occur each year in or around Tokyo, and they harbour at their core a sacred banquet to which the gods are invited. Once the religious ceremonies are over, however, there are processions, games, dances, songs, shows and contests to entertain the gods and cheer the faithful. *Matsuri* have a wonderfully liberating effect on the people who participate in them. They lose their stiffness, they become relaxed, happy. They feel at peace with themselves and the gods. Without knowing it perhaps, they are drawing upon deep well-springs from which a great part of their culture—not just their religion—flows. And this is the moment to listen for those voices of the past that Hisako says are all around.

The odd, yet fascinating thing about the Shinto religion is that it is poor in systematic thought and theology; it shuns intellectualization. It depends for its survival upon a whole body of experience, spiritual and perceptual, transmitted from one generation to the next by means of symbols, art, music, the cult of nature, poetry and ritual—all the "voices" of *matsuri*, all the things that combine to make these festivals so fascinating for a foreigner such as myself.

Hisako often comes up with precious scraps of information or stray hints that shed light on Tokyo's past and help illuminate its present. She was the first to tell me about the *Ta-asobi* ritual. This archaic fertility rite, a direct survival of the agricultural civilization that flourished in "Tokyo before Tokyo", takes place every winter in a small dilapidated old shrine situated in the northern section of the city.

I attended it as a result of a chance meeting with an old English friend who is a brilliant architect. Tokyo has become a great centre for international congresses, meetings, conventions, symposia of every imaginable type and size. There are hundreds every year; the Japanese love organizing these gatherings of doctors, economists, businessmen, retailers, musicologists, scientists, philosophers, scuba divers, stamp collectors, jugglers and what not. They move people about by the hundreds with the precision of ballet troupes and with that genuine Confucian delight in ceremonies. It so happened, that, at the time the *Ta-asobi* was to be held, architects from all over the world were convening in Tokyo; but apart from noticing that there were signs everywhere welcoming them to the city, I paid their congress little notice.

I ran into my architect friend at an afternoon reception that was held at the British Embassy, a place that combines a delightful period atmosphere

Glossary

Key Japanese words and phrases that recur in this book, although defined or explained as they occur in the text, have been assembled in this glossary as a convenient reference source for the reader.

Bunka—culture, civilization.

Bunraku—puppet theatre, developed in Osaka in the 17th Century and now performed all over Japan.

Cho—small city neighbourhood, anything from several hundred houses and buildings to fewer than a hundred.

Daimyo—"Great Name", feudal lord.

Danchi—cheap block of flats.

Edo—"Mouth of the River", Tokyo's old name.

Edokko—"Son of Tokyo", third generation Tokyoite.

Futon—bedding, bedquilt.

Gaijin—"Outside person", foreigner.

Ie—house, home or household; in old times, an *ie* consisted of the master, his family, servants, house, land and possessions. Although the tradition is dying out, the *ie* survives, transformed, in the paternalistic Japanese corporation.

Jubako—a tier of lacquer boxes, used to store picnic food.

Kabuki—traditional popular theatre, which originated in the early 17th Century when it included female performers. Because of scandal surrounding the actresses, boys were soon cast for the female roles. From the mid-17th Century onward, men have taken all the parts.

Kaisha—company, corporation (heavily paternalistic).

Kami—deity, god, superior being, spirit.

Kanji—from *Kan* (Chinese), *ji* (letters); the individual signs of ideograms in Japanese script, borrowed from the Chinese c. 5th Century.

Kimon—"The Demon's Gate", dread north-eastern point of the compass from which evil spirits supposedly emanated.

Kurisamasu—Christmas.

Makoto—sincerity, faithfulness, honesty; a key Japanese moral value.

Matsuri—festival, once mainly Shinto (Japan's indigenous faith), now used indiscriminately to describe a variety of lively occasions.

Meiji—"Enlightened Rule", posthumous name of Emperor Mutshito (1850-1912); also applied to spectacular period of modernization and Westernization that occurred between 1868 and 1912.

Noh—a refined blend of narrative music and dance developed in the 14th Century from aristocratic and rural traditions. The actions of the masked dancers have profound symbolic meaning.

Ojigi—bow, obeisance.

O-shogatsu—"The Honoured Standard Month", the New Year.

Pachinko—pinball game. Invented in Nagoya after the war, *pachinko* remains immensely popular throughout Japan.

Ronin—masterless samurai, or warrior.

Saké—rice wine, usually served warm.

Samurai—"One who serves" (militarily), the retainer of a *daimyo* lord; in a more general sense, the military class.

Seppuku—suicide by disembowelment (*hara-kiri* is the more common term for the same thing).

Shibui—originally "astringent, rough", now a term of aesthetic appreciation meaning quiet, sober, tasteful, elegantly simple.

Shinto—Japan's native religion, basically worship of the divine element in nature; a cult of ancestor spirits.

Shitamachi—"downtown", or lower town. Low-lying ward of Tokyo that grew largely on land reclaimed from Tokyo Bay; inhabited mostly by artisans and merchants.

Shogun—military governor. Originally the title was *Seii Taishogun* (Supreme Chief Who Subdues the Barbarians). Although appointed at first by the Emperor to keep the peace, the shogun became a kind of "temporal king", *de facto* ruler of Japan until the restoration of the Emperor's full powers in 1868.

Shushi—small cakes of rice containing fish, often wrapped in seaweed.

Tatami—rectangular straw mats used to cover floors in a traditional Japanese home.

Tenno—"Celestial king", the Emperor.

Tokonoma—alcove in the home for displaying flower arrangements, pictures and so on traditionally includes a small Buddhist altar.

Tashiki—residence, palace, villa.

Zoni (or **o-zoni**)—typical soup prepared for the first meal on New Year's Day. There are many recipes, but all contain *mochi*: white cakes of pounded rice.

with an auspicious address: Number One of Number One Town. There, standing among the guests, was George. He is tall and tweedy, and his mischievous face, with pursed lips, never fails to remind me of those enigmatic stone monuments on Easter Island. "I'm here on this architects' circus," he told me, "and it's my first visit to Japan—I'm very excited!" He made no bones about wanting to cut "that highfalutin congress". As we were talking, I remembered suddenly that it was February 12, the day of the *Ta-asobi* festival that Hisako had told me about. I was certain that George would enjoy it. "Are you ready for a longish trip, some discomfort and a lot of cold?," I asked him. He said he didn't mind in the least, and off we went. After a long ride in the underground, another on the elevated railway and yet another on a suburban tram (all during the rush-hour, with crowds floating like tide water through tunnels and corridors, up and down gangways), we reached the small station of Tobu-Nerima nearly an hour later. Here, Tokyo can be caught in the very act of devouring its countryside. The city has spread like a hungry lichen: warrens of wooden houses and shacks gradually, sneakily cover old paddyfields and are at once transformed into slatternly, overcrowded neighbourhoods. But that process has been going on for years.

Now another process is at work, a far more ominous one: powerful real estate companies are buying up great tracts of land, bringing in their bull-dozers to level the hills and fill in the hollows, and then building row upon row of *danchi*—cheap apartment houses—eight or ten storeys high. When we found our little shrine it seemed in danger of being swallowed up by the advancing *danchi*. Some fine old trees managed to survive intact from the time when the shrine must have been a local sanctuary of the Shinto faith way out in the fields.

The usual festive signs put up for a *matsuri* were few and poor: a scattering of lanterns in front of the houses and a few coloured paper flowers—as if people cared little, or no more, for the atavistic rites that were about to take place there. And for what, after all, was fertility being requested? The paddyfields had been buried beneath cement and asphalt. Yet beyond the traditional torii gate, on the level court before the rickety shrine, a few old men in white kimonos were solemnly preparing for their ceremony. This particular *matsuri* takes place after dark, and now the sun, setting beyond a cluster of leafless trees above the bony profiles of buildings, gave way gradually to one of Tokyo's brilliantly clear winter evenings, with bracing air and blue skies, and a fiendishly cold wind straight out of Siberia.

The old men stared at us. There were no visitors, so what were these two stray *gaijin*—foreigners—doing here? Behind a small desk in an open wooden building near the main shrine squatted a rather solemn person wearing a dark coat, a necktie, and an incongruous yellow ski cap on his head. On a piece of paper hanging from his table, the characters for *uketsuke*—reception—were written in a clumsy and uncertain hand.

For a moment I wondered what to do, and then I fished out one of my visiting cards (essential for social contacts in Japan). I presented it to the old man, explaining that my friend and I were very interested in the subject of *matsuri* generally and in his festival in particular. Would he let us watch the proceedings and favour us with his guidance and explanation?

His dour expression vanished: he smiled, looked very pleased, and asked us to climb up on the high, wooden floor and take a seat on a cushion near a large brazier. A girl was called and appeared from somewhere, bringing tea. "I am Suzuki," the old man said. "I am a teacher at a school near here, and my family has been connected with this shrine for generations. We still manage to hold our *Ta-asobi*, but how long will it last? It is a very ancient ritual. It means a lot to farmers, but there are few farmers left around here. It must have been very trying for you to come so far on such a cold evening: get nearer to the brazier." So Mr. Suzuki, who minutes before had looked rather like a jaundiced Spanish saint painted by El Greco, now, with a face full of smiles and bowing right and left, changed into an ancient ivory carving come to life.

The men in white were busy round four tall bamboo stakes that had been planted in the level ground at the corners in front of the shrine: a slender straw rope encircling the stakes established the boundary of a sacred space some five metres square. At its centre stood a large drum: "This is our symbolic nursery and paddyfield, our holy paddyfield," Mr. Suzuki explained, "and do not forget that in the olden times this was New Year's Day. It is a great moment if you think about it. Spring is just about to start. Trees, bushes, grasses are about to blossom. It is now that the gods descend from their abodes in the mountains and make their home in the fields. All sorts of evil spirits and malignant goblins roam around. The gods are busy fighting them. We should entertain them. This is what the *Ta-asobi* is all about."

Fortunately there were still some old men who knew every detail of the ritual, and we were duly introduced to them. One, whose name was Koizumi-san, wore a ceremonial kimono (actually a simple white duster hung loosely over his rustic clothes); he joined us for a moment, warming his hands over the brazier. He must have been about 70, a wrinkled, grinning gnome straight out of a print by Hokusai or Hiroshige. "Koizumi-san used to farm around here," Mr. Suzuki said, a little patronizingly. "Now there are *danchi* buildings over his fields, ha ha! Well, he became rich selling the land. That's not bad is it? But he's a farmer in spirit; he'll always be a farmer. He knows everything about the ritual. He learned the rules from our elders when a *Ta-asobi* was still an occasion and hundreds of people crowded around the shrine from all the neighbouring villages. This evening Koizumi-san acts as Elder Father of the Rice and leads the ritual."

A boy brought some *saké*—the Japanese rice wine—in a beer bottle that had been immersed in boiling water to heat it, and the hot drink was

Foxes, traditional messengers of the rice-god Inari, flank the steps leading to the torii gates of one of Inari's many shrines. Folk belief holds that Inari descends from the mountains each spring to ensure a good crop and returns after harvest time. In modern Tokyo he is also considered as the patron god of merchants.

offered round. We all sipped with relish and it warmed our freezing bodies.

"Oeh, oeh, Koizumi-san," called Mr. Suzuki. "You take a sip with us and pass some over to the men." Grinning and bowing, Koizumi-san came around, swigged a whole glass of *saké* without blinking, then returned with the bottle in his hand to the sacred enclosure.

By now it was completely dark. Stars shone brilliantly in the black sky. A jet aircraft, hissing and thundering and its red lights throbbing, passed fairly low above our heads. Someone lit a harsh electric bulb above the sacred enclosure. "In the old days we had *taimatsu*—real pine tree torches full of resin," Mr. Suzuki told us. "But now they have become too expensive." All the actors were ready—Koizumi, the gnome, as "Elder Father of the Rice", another old man as "Lesser Father of the Rice", followed by five or six men in white who were to mime the work in the fields, using symbolic hoes and scythes. There were also some small boys, wearing curious caps on their heads, who would act as *saotome*—the girls who transplant the rice seedlings from nursery to field in summer. Most of the participants looked miserably cold and dejected. There was something pathetic in this forlorn gathering of mummers on a windy night in a depressing city suburb: men and boys moved about as if they were taking part in a last, melancholy stand against an inexorable fate.

One of the elders started thumping on the large drum in a typical Japanese rhythm, slow but somehow full of magic life. The actors took their allotted places. Koizumi-san chanted an ancient invocation in a strange high-pitched voice: "This is the rice nursery of the Great Celestial Luminous God, the hallowed centre of ten thousand villages to the east, ten thousand to the west, ten thousand also to the south and the north, and in the centre too. Fifty thousand villages in all. So, respectfully, we may start to pray."

Presently another old man in white took hold of a twig decorated with a large rice dumpling and imitated, in delightful pantomime, the act of tilling the nursery, to the accompaniment of thumps from the great drum. When the seed bed had been carefully prepared, it was time to start sowing the rice. Old Koizumi raised his voice, and chanting with astonishing vigour for someone so bent and gnarled, announced: "Ye lords of the Manor, ye chiefs and gentlemen, ye farmers old and young, ye lords of the gods (the Shinto priests), ye ladies, wives, children, tillers of the fields; let us all joyfully sow the blessed rice . . . hoeeee." While Koizumi was singing his prayer, an assistant took hold of a square wooden box and mimed the act of scattering the rice in all directions over the sacred enclosure.

Although the wind and cold had worsened, people seemed to be waking up, warming up. Children crowded around the mummers, jumping and clapping their hands. A group of pretty girls—obviously on their way back from the public bath, with green plastic basins under their arms and towels turbaned on their heads—stood giggling near the torii or gateway. Mr.

To the faithful, these decorative-looking objects hanging outside a Shinto shrine are infused with clear, spiritual meaning. The rope defines the boundaries of a sacred area; the paper strips symbolize offerings and purity; and the bell is rung to summon the attention of the gods.

Suzuki offered around more and more of his excellent *saké*. Now, proper small porcelain bottles had arrived with neat little cups.

George was having a splendid time; he was managing to conduct a sort of non-verbal conversation with Mr. Suzuki, by means of gestures, grins, grunts and hand-clapping. Every now and then Koizumi-san came up for refills and gulped them down with the humorous, incredibly elegant movements and gestures of an accomplished actor in an ancient farce.

As we were finishing off another round of hot *saké*, the men in white began dancing around grotesquely and making a curious noise by rapping and scraping hollow bamboo sticks. "Look! Now they are chasing the birds away!" Mr. Suzuki cried out. They were nimble, agile, alert; age meant nothing. They moved with the perfect assurance, the uniformity and gestures one generally expects from a trained ballet corps. One man put the rough, primitive—although very effective—mask of an ox on his face and was then led around the enclosure. The symbolic field was thus ploughed and levelled, then enriched with invisible fertilizer.

The time had now come for the greatest of all events, one which is celebrated in reality with carousal and merrymaking all over Japan during the months of June and July: the transplanting of the rice seedlings from their nurseries to the open fields. Someone led the four little boys, playing the roles of girls, to the sacred enclosure. Amid great laughter and many shrieks, the men tossed them in the air, over the large drum. Our little *matsuri*, which had started on such a pathetic note of diffidence and shivers, was warming up prodigiously. Mr. Suzuki, who had thrown away his skier's cap and his necktie, was all red in the face and looked terribly dishevelled, but he made us feel wonderfully relaxed as he became ever more hospitable. He seemed to have inexhaustible reserves of his exquisite drink. Two young men came along with real *taimatsu* torches; a man followed them, holding in his hands a basket with a large pillow on which someone had painted a funny moonlike face. "Oeh, oeh, look!" Mr. Suzuki shouted to me. "That is Yonebo, the Rice Child. He's fine isn't he?" We all laughed. We felt deliciously comfortable and vague. Suddenly a fat person wearing the mask of a girl with a cushion round the waist to suggest pregnancy, came on the scene. There was much excitement; children clapped and yelled. Old Koizumi—red now as boiled beetroot after all the *saké*, yet still able to maintain his balance—shouted in a shrill, stylized voice, "Come out!" Someone else, with a mask on his face, jumped into the arena under the harsh electric light and embraced the "girl". The two then started a ludicrous dance to the accompaniment of furious bangs on the drum. There was much commotion and gales of boisterous laughter.

The mime became more and more grotesque, with a clearly sexual significance, but the instinctively stylized gestures were somehow purified of all vulgarity. The symbolism of this ancient dance perfectly suited the spirit of our *matsuri*, a centuries-old festival born out of man's unsophisticated wonder at the miracle of life resurgent with the New Year, redolent of his longing for abundance, for plentiful harvests. It was imbued with that magical belief that the fire of sex, aroused in human beings, can transmit its warmth to soil and seed, and enrich and arouse the dormant cycle of fertility. Then, abruptly, the dance was over. The men in white were pretending to gather the harvest. Our *matsuri* was drawing to an end in a wonderful atmosphere of gaiety.

The crowd had become fairly large and there were many young people milling around. Those who were inebriated wandered here and there with that air of childlike innocence into which most Japanese tend to fall when they've drunk too much. A man nonchalantly relieved himself against a bush. In the icy sky, another aeroplane passed above our heads, drowning us all for a moment in its roar. My thoughts wandered up there to the human load inside the great metal bird: tourists, businessmen, politicians, scientists, artists—some of them perhaps participants in other international congresses, all of them getting ready to land in "fabulous Tokyo". Soon they would be reaching their hotel castles of steel and glass, monstrous *machines à vivre* hiding miles and miles of tubes and wires in their walls, electronically nerved and brained to regulate their own heat, water, moisture, light, power, time, finances. I imagined these new visitors wandering among the warm, scented, carpeted fields of the hotels' shopping arcades, where other fertilities, other harvests are celebrated: bushels of cultivated pearls, shelf-loads of cameras, radios, television sets, tape recorders, calculators, musical instruments, toys. There would be food, drink, silk, novelties—a prodigious abundance of things. These new arrivals would move in a world infinitely different and distant from that of Yonebo the Rice Child, of the Elder Father of Rice. But was it so different

Celebrating an autumn festival featuring ancient rain-making dances, a spry Tokyo grandfather and his wonderstruck descendant (above) wear headbands that are souvenirs of the occasion. The spectacular Phoenix dances (right), held annually, are performed by boys, who provide their own rhythms on the drum as they leap and whirl about it. Some of the dancers are wearing helmets in the shape of the mythical Ho-o bird, or phoenix.

after all? Or was there perhaps a subtle continuity between these two aspects of the city?

I believe there is a link. The link is Shintoism, with its cult of life and fertility, its positive, affirmative, energetic, vital view of the world. Underlying this faith—even in Tokyo—is a reverence for nature as the ultimate criterion of truth, of goodness and beauty, an absolute in its own right. In Japan one is rarely confronted with those cleaving dualisms that typify Western thought: God and man, creator and creature, spirit and matter, body and soul, good and evil, nature and supernatural reality, the sacred and profane. In Shinto, men, the world and the gods all belong to what is essentially a single vital continuum.

This attitude no doubt engenders the Japanese pragmatism that had so amazed me when I saw a new Tokyo growing up from the ruins right after the war. The world being essentially divine, significant events must therefore be a form of revelation; success is thus proof of virtue, of harmony with the inner workings of nature, a minor "mandate of Heaven". This pragmatism surfaces everywhere in Tokyo, in all of Japan; in attitudes to body, food, drink, sex, money, death, work, business, play and politics. And it is there in *matsuri*.

The *Ta-asobi*—the Paddyfield Mime—is, of course, only a shadow of its former self. But other *matsuri* preserve their ancient vigour and their following, and the Phoenix dances held at the Spring-Sun Shrine (Kasuga-Jinja) near Fussa at the western edge of Tokyo is one of them. This *matsuri* takes place each autumn and is an invitation to the gods to bestow rain on the ripening rice. I had long heard about the Phoenix dances, but I had never seen them, and I determined this time to do so. However, rather than attend them with another Westerner, I decided to invite a Japanese friend—a young woman. I was curious to see what responsive chord, if any, they would strike in her.

I think I noticed Yaeko for the first time at a concert. Nobody could fail to notice her. She was quite extraordinary even for Tokyo: very small, young, ravishingly pretty, dressed in a strange kimono with an archaic flavour, and she seemed always to be waving around—at every movement of her head—her prodigiously long, blue-black hair. She looked demure and secretive, smiling most of the time as if to herself. When she spoke to me, her eyes blinked furiously and she seemed to be saying: "I'm so weak, so stupid, please tell me what to do." In reality, of course, Yaeko is shrewd, brilliantly intelligent, and as tough as nails. She writes poetry and reads voraciously in several languages. She sounds too good to be true—but Tokyo offers everything, every imaginable combination of human attributes, every refinement and combination of refinements.

Yaeko lives in a large, old, decaying house in the purest Japanese style, surrounded by a garden full of weeds, together with her idle, lazy, refined parents, both elegantly going to pieces among the last shreds of what must once have been a considerable fortune. She insisted that we go to the Phoenix dances in the family car, with the family's old retainer-chauffeur at the wheel. Yaeko had donned a pair of bluish slacks and piled all her hair on top of her head. She looked atrocious and I fear she noticed my criticizing look when we met. All during the trip she was withdrawn. Then we arrived at the shrine and she lit up.

Signs of a *matsuri* in progress were visible all over the place. The day was fine, sunny, warm. All the houses had gaily coloured paper lanterns and flowers above the entrance doors; banners with large and auspicious ideograms flapped in the breeze; children ran about in striped or dappled *yukata*—the light summer kimono. Waves of music produced by flutes and drums were carried on the breeze. Stalls selling sweets, drinks, toys, amulets, horoscopes, small Shinto altars to be set up in the home, cheap cameras and flashlights, plastic masks for children and spare bicycle parts were aligned along the path leading to the shrine.

The Spring-Sun Shrine was a modest structure, barely more than an old barn. Such simplicity, however, is not to be taken as a sign of neglect; the Japanese have generally considered Nature more important than architecture, a visible manifestation of divinity. There are some Shinto shrines in Japan of great—even extraordinary—dignity, artistry and beauty, but more often than not the "god's palace" seems to be dwarfed by a grove of ancient, awe-inspiring trees, or perhaps by a waterfall. And sometimes a shrine is completely overshadowed by a noble mountain, by the crags of some mysterious gorge, or by the majesty and immensity of the sea itself: the essential elements that inspire men, give them spiritual nourishment, invite them to meditation or to communion with invisible presences around him. The Spring-Sun Shrine's location had been chosen with care: a secluded nook at the foot of a range of hills, where the paddyfields gave way to the remnants of a wood that in old times may well have been an awesome forest.

As we climbed the steep flight of stone steps leading from the torii gate to a wide, level space in front of the shrine, a purification rite was starting. At the top three or four Shinto priests stood facing us. One, clad in a kimono of the purest blue, looked like the chief celebrant; the others had on simple white gowns. There was also a young shrine maiden—a quiet, plump beauty of serious demeanour, dressed in a long, red skirt over her immaculate kimono. The high priest held in his hands a wooden wand with a crown of white paper tassels.

Some 30 or 40 men—most of them rather old, most of them obviously farmers with weather-beaten, bronzed faces, and all in their Sunday best—stood in front of the celebrants, awestruck, at near-military attention and in perfect silence, looking towards the sanctuary. Many had visited the barber a few days, or hours, before; the white napes of necks rising from coat collars were prominently visible, a detail which, at least for me, seemed

Buried under a pile of heavy bales of rice that has been topped by a wooden mortar, one man fans himself to convey his lack of concern, while two others pound cooked rice into rice cake. Such displays of strength, once a tradition among dockside warehousemen, are still performed as festival entertainment, although the participants nowadays are more likely to be amateur body-builders—or even professional entertainers—than workers.

mute testimony to an extraordinary earnestness and sincerity. "Beware, foreigner," the white napes seemed to say, "this is no frivolous merry-making, but a moment of genuine religious communion with the great unseen. Tread respectfully on the hallowed ground." The priest waved his wand many times right and left, and the husky men dipped their heads far down. As soon as the purification rite was over, priests and congregation crowded into the shrine, where the high priest chanted a prayer in a high-pitched voice of singular beauty.

This particular *matsuri*, with its religious ceremonies and its dances, must be as old as the Paddyfield Mime, perhaps even older. While it is intended to invoke rain, there is always a risk of too much rain; and a storm could damage the burgeoning rice, since this is the time of year when typhoons blow in from the sea. So care must be taken.

The prayer began: "We bow respectfully twice, and with deep reverence we pray. The Dragon-god favours us with rain, but keeps away the wind. Today all of us unite—old men and young men—to pray for rain. May the black clouds over yonder mountains bring us shiny lightning and rain, within limits not harmful—and sooner than our voices reach heaven. Let us pray for long ears of five grains, for a whole horse-load of long-eared grain. If there is abundance of grains to be measured by bounteous basketfuls, then we may store the harvest in our granaries with joy. Hoooo! Respectfully we pray. . . ."

The family retainer-chauffeur, an impenetrable old man straight out of the Meiji past, stood at attention behind us with Yaeko's camera and the lunch basket in his hands. As the ceremony developed, offerings of fruit, *saké*, fish, rice, vegetables, all neatly arranged on diminutive red lacquer trays, were lifted from a table and handed over by the shrine maiden to the high priest, who deposited them with deep obeisances on the altar at the far end of the shrine. The gods had been invited to descend from their mysterious abodes to participate in a ceremonial banquet with the faithful. But although the feast was the real heart of this *matsuri*, few people were present: a purely religious ritual, it was far from spectacular. Visitors were waiting for the dances that would follow later. The high priest chanted again, his voice emerging from the open shrine and then lost among the branches of the old cypress trees.

Later on it amused me to tell Yaeko how that great Italian *matsuri*, the annual Palio of Siena, functions in very much the same way. Originally there was a simple ceremonial offering of candles to the Madonna in the city's cathedral; then someone, centuries ago, came up with the brilliant idea of holding races to entertain the people. Now crowds of Italians and foreigners alike visit Siena in summer for the colourful horse races, but hardly anybody knows that the ancient religious ritual from which the Palio sprung still takes place the day before, in the background. The only difference between Italy and Japan, in this respect, is that the races are held to amuse the people rather than the Madonna, who presumably has heavenly social engagements of her own, while the *matsuri* events are there for the enjoyment of men and gods together.

But now a procession of some 15 or 20 dancers and musicians appeared at the foot of the stairs. A few minutes later the dancers took up positions around the level space in front of the shrine. The first dance was performed by a number of small boys clad in blue gowns, with yellow sashes around their waists and straw sandals on their feet. These little *yakko* (slaves or pages of the gods) were made up with a bold red blot on each cheek and a firm white line straight down the nose. They danced in a circle, alternatively holding in their lifted hands a white fan or a wooden toy sword and from time to time they stopped to recite some lines in a stylized diction, as child actors do in the traditional *Kabuki* plays. At the centre of the circle stood a large drum on which an old man was beating with two short sticks, producing one of those typical Japanese rag rhythms that invite the body irresistibly to move and to dance.

Yaeko observed the pageantry with rapture, exclaiming often, "*Bellissimo!*" Then she turned to me with one of those angelic smiles that always seemed to precede a comment that was definitely naughty: "Think how Yoshimitsu would have enjoyed it all" she said. I failed to catch the erudite allusion.

"The great shogun Yoshimitsu, in Kyoto, six hundred years ago", she explained for the benefit of her befuddled foreign escort. "It must have been something like this when he spotted Zeami, a 12-year-old actor, a budding genius. Yoshimitsu became Zeami's lover and patron. And Zeami later practically created the Noh drama for Yoshimitsu's illustrious court.

"Look! What ravishing dolls! We ancient Japanese knew a good thing when we saw it." When she noticed my reaction, she asked mischievously, "What's wrong with little boys?" Yaeko loves to move about in a vague aura of scandal. "I wonder if the little *yakko* pages are required to be virgins?" she went on, with the complete detachment of an anthropologist. "But, after all, what does a virgin mean in the case of a male, eh?"

The subject was dropped as the pages filed out and eight or ten Phoenix dancers leapt splendidly into the area. Immediately it was another world. The dancers were youths clad, as the pages had been, in blue gowns with straw sandals on their feet, but wearing on their heads as a distinctive crest an extraordinary brass helmet in the shape of a winged bird: the mythical *Ho-oh*—the phoenix, a most auspicious and noble creature. The children's dance had been simple, measured, gentle, slightly effeminate. The youths' Phoenix dance was virile and pugnacious, yet elegant, precise, cutting—like the blade of a sword. The youths leapt martially around the large drum in intricate figures of extraordinary vigour, with sudden halts during which they struck poses of sculptural beauty—all to the accompaniment of fierce yells and crashing percussions on the drum, timed with breathtaking precision. The dance produced an overwhelming impression of brilliant energy, exquisitely controlled and refined by age-old tradition. "The dance is miraculous in its own right", we were told by a grinning, wrinkled old man. "It keeps away illnesses and brings the right rains; it protects us all. . . ." Yaeko looked immensely thrilled.

Not far from the shrine an empty wooden bench stood under a tree. Yaeko and I stopped there for our picnic lunch. The chauffeur produced a fine old *jubako* case—a tall wooden box, lacquered in black with minute golden scenes of country life, containing in its various compartments a delicious choice of *sushi*—small rice cakes with raw fish fillets. We ate our *sushi* slowly. The shrine, the woods, the distant fields, all were quiet now. "There are occasions," Yaeko said thoughtfully, "when eating rice may be a sort of holy communion. It is rather like bread in the West, no?

"Rice follows us everywhere as a nation," she went on between bites, "and as individuals. When we get married, it is the nine sips of *saké* that sanctify the union of man and woman. And rice is offered to the dead, and to Buddhas, and to Kami, the Shinto gods."

All true. What few people realize is that the entire sacred cycle of rice cultivation is re-enacted symbolically every year, in the innermost heart of Tokyo, by the Emperor himself. With his own hands he cares for a diminutive field in the gardens of the Imperial Enclosure. These rites are rather secret and mysterious: one doesn't hear much about them, and perhaps that is as it should be. They are like a precious flame perpetually burning, something connecting the tumultuous present with the mythological past, through work and everyday food.

I love walking through the centre of Tokyo, with all those gigantic buildings towering over me, banks and headquarters of powerful corporations, where busy men sit near tremendous computers making plans that may affect the world economy, while over there, beyond a moat and a wall and a cluster of trees, the Emperor himself is tilling his field, or sowing it, or transplanting seedlings, or reaping sheaves of luscious yellow rice that will be cleaned, boiled and offered—still rich with perfume—to the gods.

Some day these secret, mysterious, ancient rites may be abolished, or transformed. The loss will be regrettable. For what other great city of the world holds at its very heart, as one of its sacred possessions, a small, authentic rice field, the symbol of all sorts of important, ancient, true, brave and beautiful things?

The City's Hidden Villages

Reflected in a blind-corner traffic mirror, a postman and a restaurant's delivery boy make their rounds in Tsukuda, one of Tokyo's secluded neighbourhoods.

Tucked away behind Tokyo's noisy main thoroughfares are dozens of small, quiet communities where sing-song cries of street pedlars replace the roar of traffic. These "villages", some in the very centre of the city, have their own baths, shrines, festivals and—although to a lessening extent nowadays—local customs. Their roots reach back centuries to the time when the city's many small wards were so self-contained that at night each locked its gates against outsiders. In our era their separateness is maintained by lanes almost too narrow for cars and by a general absence of street names—discouraging for visitors, but providing a sense of cosy isolation to the inhabitants, who know all the area's nooks and byways. The intimate atmosphere helps to make life tolerable amid the frenzied pace of an otherwise overwhelming metropolis.

An old man shuffling along a familiar lane pauses for breath. In former times local communities helped look after the aged in need, but nowadays it is the State, more often than the neighbourhood, that cares for the indigent.

Elbow on a pillow, a man in a window relaxes with a newspaper beside his lovingly tended garden—a few square yards between house and roadway.

Where old-style houses of wood, bamboo and tile jostle each other for every inch of space, a woman finds a tiny patch of sun in which to hang her washing.

Living behind walls of wood and paper, people expect and get little privacy.

Within a mile of the Ginza in the bustling heart of Tokyo, a back-alley chicken coop provides the world's second largest city with a delightfully rural touch.

A boy peeks through the cane fence surrounding a garden in one of the city's old districts. Such see-through fences, characteristic of "village" Tokyo, politely delineate space while preserving a neighbourhood's intimate charm.

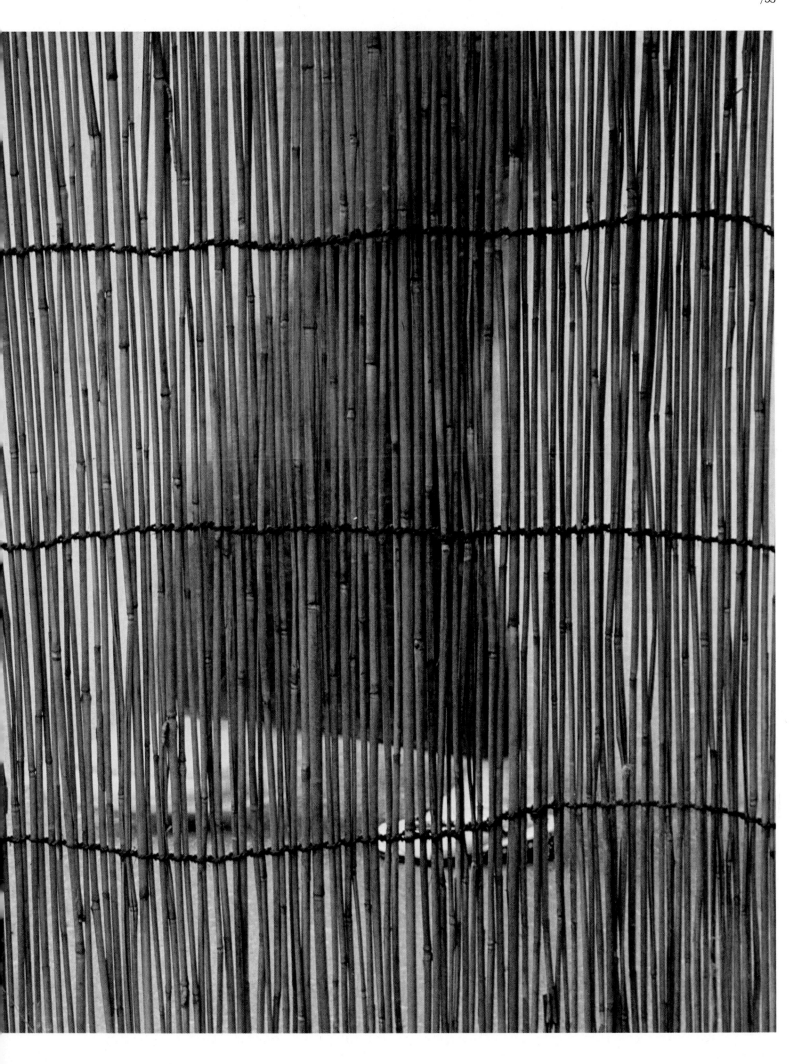

3

The People of Edo

Direct contact with the physical past is a commonplace of most Western cities, where the past is preserved in stone. I have a Roman friend whose house—ex-chapel, ex-temple of Bacchus—was built on the Appian Way about 2,000 years ago. In Japan's timber-based culture—and in a fire-prone city like Tokyo—the monuments of yesterday all too often go up in smoke. Yet, in the end, only relics are consumed; much else that is ancient survives. A Westerner visiting Tokyo is likely to be overwhelmed by the modern city: the language barrier is bad enough, the "ideographic curtain" worse, and both keep hidden from him the preoccupation of so many of the inhabitants with all that has gone before them. But live in Tokyo a while and the past looms large.

Never have I felt closer to it or more comforted by it than when I rented for a year a small house in Rokubancho—which roughly translates as Town Number Six—quite near to the Imperial Enclosure. I still regard as something of a miracle the fact that I could dwell right in the heart of Tokyo, a half hour's walk from the central area, yet feel miles away and at times even in the countryside.

Rokubancho lies on relatively high land, where long ago the lower orders of feudal society had their quarters, and it has never been heavily built up. Here and there, of course, one sees the usual concrete blocks of offices and apartments, and an occasional, improbable television mast—looking like a gigantic tropical insect. But it is also possible to get lost in Rokubancho's quiet alleys, flanked by low houses, by schools and temples, by unobtrusive villas with trees bursting over their garden walls. Cars are few, the streets being narrow and full of sudden turns; and people generally walk. The sound of their footsteps echoes from the walls. It is quiet enough to hear distinctly, on a late afternoon after school is finished for the day, a melancholy call that is constantly repeated: the long-drawn-out *Yaki-imoooooo* advertising roast sweet-potatoes, a Japanese delight. The cry comes from an old man pushing a steaming, wheeled contraption that suggests a mobile samovar, and the sound carries so because he is yelling it through a little electronic loudspeaker. This typical Tokyo conjunction—the ultra-modern gadget and the street-cry as old as the city—is enhanced by the children, entirely modern in dress and appearance, who burst from their wholly traditional houses to buy the old man's treat.

How happy I was in Town Number Six! From there I could plunge into the whirlpool of Tokyo as if into my own swimming-pool, and sport in the absurd and stimulating confusion of its streets, shops, theatres, bars,

Weekend crowds walk in autumn rain through the tree-filled gardens leading to the Meiji Shrine, a favourite place for family outings. Built in 1920, the shrine commemorates Emperor Hirohito's grandfather, the Emperor Meiji whose reforms in the 19th Century initiated Japan's emergence into the modern world.

temples, libraries, restaurants, markets, universities, turkish baths, department-stores, museums. And when tired or satiated, I could drift back to Town Number Six as to a hermit village—to talk with friends, read, listen to music, write or just sit quietly thinking.

I found the house entirely by chance, looking through the advertisements in a local paper. It was a modest two-storeyed structure of timber, built in an unpretentious Japanese style—the sort of place still to be seen everywhere in the suburbs, although it is disappearing in more central areas. I reached it by following a long, silent alley up to wooden sliding doors. A ring on the old-fashioned bell gave access to a little garden, lovingly tended and looking like an embroidery—with precisely spaced bushes and flowers and miniature *bonsai* or dwarf trees in rectangular pots.

The house itself stood tightly hugged between two others of similar design. The kitchen, dining-room and Japanese bathroom were on the ground floor, and upstairs there were a Western-style studio and a large, uncompromisingly Japanese room with *tatami* mats for rest and sleep. Unostentatious as it was, this particular room had been finished without regard to expense: fine wood and excellent workmanship were evident throughout, especially in the post marking the *tokonoma* recess (a corner in which the Japanese hang a prized picture or set a flower arrangement or some valuable ornament). It was delightful to find such restrained sumptuousness in a setting marked otherwise by practical economy.

The house belonged to a Mr. and Mrs. Miura (he was a retired musician and writer) and, naturally, upon entering it, a guest was expected to take off his shoes. This requirement can be curiously irritating to a foreigner visiting Tokyo, at least in the beginning. One may read in diaries, or see in old prints, how the irrational pride of Westerners compelled them to ignore what their hosts considered an indignity, causing them to force their booted way like barbarians into houses and temples. It is easy to get used to the custom, however, and to appreciate its significance as a symbolic exclusion of the outside world. It seems to confer on the home into which the guest is welcomed an extraordinary sense of intimacy and security. Here, in a secluded world of order and silence, the dirt, noise, pointless-ness and brutality of the street are left at the front door clinging to the discarded shoes. On this count, ancient Shinto ideas of contamination and desecration by dirt accorded with practical good sense: the roads may now be asphalted and the gesture therefore largely one of ritual, but in times past they were deep in mud or dust, according to the season. In some parts of Japan, footwear is deliberately worn in a house during the removal of the dead for cremation or burial—so recalcitrant Westerners may at times give greater offence than they know entering with their shod feet inside the house.

Another typically Japanese arrangement in my little house—in spite of its severely restricted space—was the separation between lavatory and

At the entrance to a simple Shinto shrine, rows of shoes—both Western lace-ups and the traditional Japanese clogs and sandals—await the return of their owners. Such line-ups are common in Japan where it is customary to remove shoes before entering homes, tea houses and family hotels as well as shrines.

bath. I think this has a symbolic importance beyond the merely fortuitous difference in approach to these two aspects of personal hygiene. It seems to me that the contempt for the body inherent in Christianity has, over the centuries, resulted in a view of the bath as no more than an unfortunate necessity, as brutish in its way as any other bodily function; and that this attitude has permitted Western builders to save space and money by making the "bathroom" do service as lavatory as well, without spiritual offence.

Truth to tell, this is also happening in modern Tokyo, where hotel bathrooms are indistinguishable from those in Washington or Edinburgh. Not so in private houses, where economics has not yet been entirely victorious over spiritual delicacy. There the act of bathing is no mere concession to the dreadful tendency of bodies to become soiled. It is, rather, an act of respect—amounting almost to worship—for the corporeal being whose worth, in Japan, is not inferior to that of the spiritual being. With its roots in ritual ablutions and purifications, bath-time in Tokyo is a pious, auspicious and above all a happy occasion, into which the intrusion of a lavatory bowl would be a barbarism, even a sacrilege.

The Japanese bathroom, however small, is a place in which to relax, to enjoy what Ruth Benedict, the American anthropologist, has called "restful indulgence", and to do it in the company of other humans. Nor is this congenial attitude confined to private bathrooms; on any afternoon you will find your local public bath full of Japanese luxuriating together in hot water, washing in a leisurely way and gossiping or exchanging news. It is a far cry from the hasty rinse behind locked doors that is all the Westerner can hope for; and it is one of the things that makes life bearable in Japan—even in a fast-tempo city like Tokyo, where people are subjected to frightful stress.

The windows on the southern side of the house looked on to Mrs. Miura's garden, while those on the opposite side opened towards the precinct of a run-down small temple surrounded by trees. The trees had been badly burned during the air raids; but their vitality could not be curtailed and they were now thick with leaves again. In their midst stood a rickety wooden pavilion, of the kind so often seen dwarfed by a tremendous cliff or waterfall in classical Chinese paintings. Nobody ever seemed to visit these grounds for religious purposes, but sometimes on Saturday afternoons a mysterious group of young revellers invaded the pavilion to drink *saké*, and to sing and laugh boisterously far into the night. I enjoyed the vicarious company of these unexplained party-makers and envied them. Nobody seemed to know or care who they were—certainly not Mrs. Miura, who had only two real interests: her garden and ghost stories.

Perhaps the revellers were ghosts, too? That would have appealed to Mrs. Miura. She was fond of telling me about O-Kiku, a beautiful serving maid who long ago had lived in the neighbourhood. Unjustly tortured and drowned by her jealous mistress on the pretext that she had stolen one of

Friends in a Tokyo public bath perch on stools to scrub themselves before entering the communal tub. They have met here daily for years, always at 5.30 a.m.

a set of ten dishes, she can still be heard—according to Mrs. Miura—desperately counting, but always stopping at nine. Then there was O-Iwa, slowly poisoned by her husband and still wandering around the district. It would not do to mock Mrs. Miura's fascination with the supernatural; it is too widespread among the Japanese for that—and Mrs. Miura herself suggested to me that the area had been left alone by land speculators because "there are too many ghosts around here". That seems to me altogether too far-fetched. And yet I never did find out who those Saturday revellers were.

Underneath the healthily pragmatic surface of Tokyo, which reflects an undoubtedly authentic preoccupation with the day-to-day activities of the business world, I have glimpsed uncanny presences, or at least a widespread belief in them. I would not myself assert that such things exist. I simply say that they flourish as beliefs and have, therefore, an influence on the life of the city while providing a subliminal access to its past.

I have spoken in the preceding chapter about Palaeo-Tokyo, or Proto-Tokyo, coming to life in festivals and rituals that express ancient collective memories. There is also what I like to call Meta-Tokyo, an imagined supernatural precursor of this great city, built in the collective unconscious of its people and a great breeder of odd circumstances—or, at the very least, odd interpretations.

Take the case of Taira Masakado, for instance, a great noble who lived a thousand years ago near where Tokyo now stands. He is still remembered with small offerings of *saké*, fruit, twigs and flowers left at the base of his memorial among the skyscrapers of central Tokyo. He is supposed to have considered himself unjustly slighted in his ambition for high office and, acting out of disappointment and anger, turned his back on Kyoto, then the capital of Japan. He built himself a power base in the east, and set himself up as an independent ruler. The Emperor could not allow this, and sent his forces to vanquish him.

The Japanese have never been able to make up their minds about Masakado. Was he an arrogant rebel? Or was he a great and tragic hero who suffered unjust persecution? In any case, such a colourful figure was bound to go on living in the imaginations of the people—especially in a country like Japan, where those who die in the fury of hatred, the throes of grief or of love, are believed by some to become spirits who demand satisfaction from, or take revenge upon, the living.

Following Masakado's death, his head was severed, pickled and sent to the Emperor for inspection. In Japanese folklore the spring at which a severed head was cleaned enjoys a particularly powerful significance. In this instance the spring apparently flowed where Tokyo's business district spreads today. For centuries, a stone pillar at the site reminded passers-by of Masakado's fate; but in the rebuilding of the city after the great earthquake of 1923, the pillar was removed to a Buddhist temple in a part of

Tokyo where space was less preciously coveted. At once unpleasant things began to happen in the central area where the monument had stood: officials died suddenly, there were accidents for which no explanation could be found, merchants became unexpectedly bankrupt. Nothing would prosper. It was not hard to attribute these, and later events to the malediction of Masakado's troubled spirit; and so a new monument, with an extravagant dedicatory inscription, was promptly set up. The spirit was appeased and does no more harm.

If I felt strongly the tug of this ancient, supernatural Tokyo while living in Town Number Six, I was aware at all times of the older Tokyo that had sprung up here 400 years ago, spreading out from what is now the Imperial Enclosure. I find it strange that a city as great as Tokyo should have taken so long to come into being. Everything about the site was right for urban growth: here was a natural port with hills that could be easily fortified, and plenty of room on the plain behind them for expansion. But the centres of Japanese culture lay to the west. To the cultivated people dwelling there, this remote and underpopulated region must have seemed lawless and dangerous frontier country. Even in Masakado's day, it was an outpost, a place to be avoided by any sensible official—a windy, lonely land to be praised only for breeding sturdy horses and tough, swaggering soldiers. But as the country's population began to swell, the area took on increasing importance. Still, it was not until the 15th Century that Tokyo really began. A minor feudal lord, Ota Dokan, planted a rudimentary castle on a bluff not far from the sea, more or less where the Imperial Palace stands today. Dokan is thus considered by some to be the founder of the city and a bronze statue at the entrance to the Metropolitan Government Building commemorates him.

Obscure enough during the succeeding century, Edo, as Tokyo was then known, was taken over on August 1, 1590—a particularly auspicious date with "eight favourable astrological conjunctions"—by an extraordinary man: Tokugawa Ieyasu (1542-1616), a powerful and up-and-coming warlord of ancient lineage. He was destined to shape the course of Japanese history and the development of Edo/Tokyo for 300 years—indeed, even up to the present day. Ieyasu (according to tradition, the first name of an historical character follows the family name) was one of Japan's most exceptional sons, a political genius and brilliant military leader. By virtue of making Edo the base of his operation, he must be acknowledged as the true founder of Tokyo. Before he established himself there, what happened in Edo was of merely local interest; afterwards anything that transpired there became a matter of national significance.

Now we must digress a moment to provide some background to the times. Until the 12th Century Japan had been governed by a line of charismatic sovereigns—the Emperors. But then in the 12th Century,

A stretch of the moat that marks the perimeter of the Imperial Enclosure mirrors an evening sky. On the wall beyond is an ancient storehouse for arrows.

effective power passed into the hands of hereditary military governors: the shoguns. Those belonging to the Ashikaga family, who ruled from the 14th Century onwards, although great patrons and protectors of art, religion and culture, were for the most part very poor administrators. By the end of the 15th Century their dynasty had lost most of its vigour and all of its power; the country was plunged into a long period of utter disorder during which competing warlords battled for land and governed the regions they conquered as independent kingdoms. In theory the authority of the Emperor was still recognized as supreme; but that sacred institution now had, in fact, only a tenuous connection with political realities.

After 1560 a great change came about. Three exceptional leaders succeeded one another within the space of a generation. Oda Nobunaga (1534-1582) gained military control over half of Japan's 66 provinces before his betrayal and death. His successor, Toyotomi Hideyoshi, consolidated and extended that control with the help of Ieyasu. When Hideyoshi died in 1598, he left a five-year-old son, Hideyori, under a regency council headed by Ieyasu, a leader not disposed to abandon his ambitions to a child. Within two years Ieyasu had manoeuvred his opponents into armed resistance, whereupon he destroyed them at the battle of Sekigahara (1600).

From that moment Ieyasu was the de facto ruler of Japan. The title of shogun, granted to him by the Emperor in 1603, was merely formal recognition of an existing situation. The form of government, and the administrative and social organizations he devised and put into effect during the 13 years of his rule survived him for more than 250 years, until 1867, through a line of 14 descendants.

The 264 years of the Tokugawa era, as it has come to be called after Ieyasu's family name (which may be translated as beneficent river) gave rise to almost all of the clichés that Westerners think of as representing the old Japan: rigorous isolation, ferocious anti-Christianism, centralized feudal administration; but it also produced spectacular development of the popular Arts and a new phase of cultural refinement. For, what Ieyasu and his descendants gave Japan was unbroken peace and strong government. Out of that stability came *Kabuki* theatre and *Bunraku* (puppet theatre), new developments in poetry and literature, woodblock prints, unsurpassed skills in such fields as lacquerwork, ceramics and textiles. And that splendidly vital and sensuous culture of the Tokugawas had its fountainhead in the great city growing up around the castle of Edo.

In spite of repeated destruction by fire and earthquake, Tokyo still bears the imprint of Ieyasu's imagination. The Imperial Enclosure at the heart of Tokyo—moats, fairy-tale turrets, park and all—was planned in outline by Ieyasu. The whole of central Tokyo—Hibiya, Yurakucho, Ginza, Nihombashi, Tsukiji—is, in a sense, the invention of Ieyasu and his descendants.

Until the early 17th Century much of the land on which central Tokyo stands lay under the shallows of the bay, and was reclaimed from them by Ieyasu and his successors. The whole of Tokyo, indeed, exists as an expression of Ieyasu's intuition: he might have chosen for his new town the old administrative capital of Kamakura, 50 miles to the south-west; but Kamakura, well-adapted for defence between its steep hills, was no place for expansion, and Ieyasu's vision was large. His view encompassed not just what he could see, but the whole of Japan; and from that stand-point Edo/Tokyo—with its hills, room for growth and easily fortified port—was in a far more advantageous position than its rival, Kyoto, and far better suited to maritime operations than Kamakura.

Nevertheless, Edo could not have been a very attractive place in 1590, when Ieyasu settled there. The castle built by Ota Dokan was in an advanced state of dilapidation, held together by planking from derelict ships and otherwise supported by a miserable village of perhaps a hundred thatched hovels. Yet, only a few years later a city of 150,000 surrounded the most splendid castle in Japan—"a place very strong," wrote Richard Cocks, an English visitor in 1616, "duble diched and ston walled about, and a league over each way. The Emperours pallis"—to mistake the shogun for the Emperor was common enough before Japan opened up to the West, so much power did the shogun hold—"is a huge thing, all the rums being gilded with gold, both over head and upon the walls, except some mixture of paintings amongst of lions, tigers, panthers, eagles, and other beasts and fowles, very lively drawn." In another four or five generations, Edo, with a population estimated at 1.3 million, had become the largest city in the world.

At night the silence around the house in Town Number Six, so redolent of Edo's past, was positively rural. The chirping of innumerable insects— which thrive in the moist summer and autumn of Japan—was much louder than the noise of the distant city, humming and breathing like the surf of some far-off ocean behind the dunes. Around dawn, a range of large birds used to perch in our trees, and wood-pigeons filled the air with a romantic moan. Mr. Miura, my landlord, was sure these creatures came from the forest inside the Imperial Enclosure close by. Perhaps to call it a forest is a bit excessive; but a section of the 284-acre enclosure is certainly kept as a wild preserve, with old trees, winding rustic paths, a brook running beneath the canopy of branches and creepers. Once or twice I have seen photographs of this secret, enchanted valley where, possibly, the only people who ever enjoy it are the Imperial Family and some old gardeners. Not that this matters, the mere thought that it exists gives me pleasure.

The name Imperial Palace for the park-like island in the centre of Tokyo always strikes me as unsatisfactory. Perhaps the word "palace" is too

A bronze statue of Ota Dokan, his warrior's bow in hand, commemorates the noble who built his castle on a bluff above Tokyo Bay in 1456. Around its ramparts grew the village of Edo that eventually became Tokyo.

vividly connected in my Italian mind with images of large, proud buildings of stone or marble or brick, elaborate and splendid, majestic celebrations of man's sovereignty. The Japanese words, *Kokyo* (emperor's residence) or *Kyujo* (castle-palace), are not essentially different; but what exists in the centre of Tokyo is both more and less than such names imply. It is not, at any rate, what you would expect. An imperial palace is there, all right: a handsome, modern building that elegantly combines traditional lines, surfaces, motifs and atmosphere with a definitely contemporary spirit and all the refinements of technology. It lies hidden among tall trees, practically invisible from the surrounding city. The Japanese embodiment of Nature tamed—a gentle composition of grass, pine trees, willow groves, boulders collected from distant mountains, ponds and hills, wood-pigeons and wild birds—seems easily to dominate the house in which the Emperor lives. When so appreciated, this large island—this giant traffic roundabout in the centre of Tokyo—becomes a triumph of delicate hints, a tracery of symbols, a landscape of suggestions and a marvel of understatement. It is Nature as the presiding deity at the core of Tokyo. And this is as it should be, for Nature occupies a central position in the Japanese civilization and is expressed as an ideal in almost every aspect of it. It is an absolute value against which everything is measured, from which everything arises and to which everything returns.

Probably Ieyasu had little to do with such subtleties. Hiroshi Bamba—my friend, the painter—is not unusual, for example, in disliking the philistinism of that far-off progenitor of the teeming city of today. But Ieyasu has plenty of admirers, too. The Japanese have not unanimously made up their minds about him. To many, Ieyasu's achievements raise him to the level of a god; and, indeed, posterity actually did deify him, making him, by Imperial decree, *Tosho Diagongen* (Great Eastern Illuminating Manifestation of Divinity), and as such he presides over the shrines at Nikko, 50 miles north of Tokyo. Others think Ieyasu should more correctly be called "Great Eastern Obscuring Manifestation of Tyranny"—a medieval Stalin—shrewd, superstitious, patient and cruel; in complete control of himself and a master of real-politik; but essentially miserly. Easy to admire, perhaps; but hard to love.

Or so one would think. But the spell of Ieyasu over many Japanese—even his detractors—is both undoubted and permanent. A romantic biography of Ieyasu, in 26 fat volumes, has been a bestseller for years. Hiroshi Bamba is peevishly critical of such adulation, which he says is the worship of mere managerial efficiency (and it is true that businessmen read Ieyasu's story in the hope of learning how to succeed). But Hiroshi is too contemptuous of worldly triumph. I asked him why one could find monuments to Dokan in Tokyo, but none to its true begetter, Ieyasu; and he told me it was because Dokan was *simpatico*—having been not only a warrior and feudal lord, but a poet, calligrapher and something of a

Buddhist sage whose realm of conquest was the spirit rather than the physical landscape and its inhabitants. Ieyasu was too brash.

An important relic of Ieyasu's time still survives, all the same. In the Imperial Enclosure, near the Hirakawa Gate to the East Garden, which is open to the public, stands an imposing rectangular dais of stone, a squat brawny mass of rough-hewn boulders. These were the foundations of the keep of Edo Castle and therefore, in a way, of Tokyo itself. The soaring 200-foot tower of wood and masonry that stood here must have been a most glorious sight in its day. It was destroyed by the disastrous fire of 1657 and was never rebuilt. The very centre of the power and intrigue of Ieyasu and his descendants lay somewhere around here, in gilded pavilions now completely vanished, although old paintings, prints and plans give us some idea of the once vast, walled city. There the shogun and his women had their apartments. A little farther down stood the splendid reception halls and offices in which the destinies of Japan were decided—each one named after some prominent floral motif in the decoration. Miles of corridors, innumerable alcoves, vast kitchens and dormitories, stables, and courts for archery contests, treasuries, libraries, a stage for Noh-drama, chapels, dungeons, gardens, ponds—everything protected by the 66 gates, 36 guardhouses and 19 corner towers, called *yagura*, the storehouses for arrows.

Here, then, is a spot permeated by the spirit of the Tokugawas and so much of what they stood for. From here that spirit drifted throughout Japan and survives in many places today as an invisible heritage, denounced as vile by some Japanese, glorified by others.

Running your hands over the rough stone vestiges of Edo castle is a rare opportunity to come into physical contact with Japan's past, although here, one's thoughts inevitably take into account the frightening amount of human toil and suffering required to build it. There was no good stone in the near-by plains; only sand, mud and volcanic cinders. Ieyasu solved that problem very typically: through his son, Hidetada, invitations were sent to the 260-or-so lords of his realm, asking them to contribute stone for the new castle. Thus, fortification of the family residence, exercise of the shogun's authority and diversion of the lords' energies away from plots and mischief were achieved at a single stroke.

Thousands of colossal stones were ferried all the way from the peninsula of Izu, one hundred miles to the west, where the only suitable quarries lay. Often there were 3,000 ships coming and going between Edo and Izu. Each ship carried no more than two stones, the largest of them called "hundred-men-stones" because that was the size of the gang needed to move them. The work lasted ten years and proceeded, as far as one can tell, with surprising smoothness. But there were times in that span when the labourers must have felt they had been dragged into something insane: 300 ships and thousands of men were lost in one stormy spell at sea; there were earthquakes, landslips, terrible accidents—and even more terrible events by no means accidental.

All large structures have a price in blood and bone, but Edo's debt to humanity is more literal than metaphorical. At that time, when something as important as a castle was being built, human sacrifices were considered essential; "human pillars" were needed to support the structure—which meant that victims were buried alive in the foundations to appease local spirits, to placate forces of evil and to ensure eternal existence for the edifice. Such sacrifices were officially forbidden, of course; but the ghastly superstition—that a building could not come into being without living flesh and blood to bless it—persisted in secret.

Very strange, mystical and horrible it must have been. Yet volunteers for these cruel rites were not lacking, which perhaps should not surprise us as we remember the suicide wartime missions in which modern Japanese willingly took part—François Caron, a French visitor to Edo early in the 17th Century, wrote about these rituals: "If a lord cause a wall to be built, either for the king or for himself, his servants oftentimes beg they might have the honour to lie under, out of a belief that what is founded upon a living man's flesh, is subject to no misfortune. This request being granted, they go with joy to the designated place, and lying down there, suffer the foundation stones to be laid upon them, which by their weight, immediately bruise and shiver them to pieces."

When workers came to restore parts of the Edo ramparts that were damaged in the 1923 earthquake, a number of skeletons were found, several of them upright with their hands joined as in prayer, and gold coins upon their shoulders and heads. How could such anguish willingly be suffered? How could it be required?

There is no undoing the past, no useful judgment to be made on its customs. One can, and must, remember with compassion and respect that, while the Imperial Enclosure preserves Nature at the centre of Tokyo, it is also founded upon blood—upon flesh "bruised and shivered to pieces". The castle has blossomed into a city, the city into a metropolis; and so, a question occurs: if the spirits of the human sacrifices who were crushed beneath Tokyo's beginnings look across the void at the urban monster they helped to spawn, do they feel pride, I wonder, or dismay?

Big Men for a Big Business

An intimidating bulk and oiled topknot identify this Tokyo giant, standing in the doorway of a gymnasium, as one of the elite of Japan's sumo wrestlers.

Sumo wrestling is among Tokyo's most popular spectator sports. Fans gladly pay out large sums for a good seat to follow every move in one of the city's big 15-day tournaments. Begun some 2,000 years ago as sacred contests—priests predicted the rice-harvest by the outcome of a match—*sumo* still involves much ritual, although reverence for tradition does not bar innovations like the use of video tape to judge close matches. The aim is to throw an opponent out of the ring or make any part of his body except his feet touch the floor. Sheer mass is, therefore, vital to the wrestlers (*sumotori*) who down huge amounts of high-calorie foods to keep their weight up. *Sumotori* usually begin their apprenticeships—which last several years—at about 15, and only a few ever achieve the stardom that brings public adulation and financial security.

At a basho (tournament) in Kokugikan Stadium, top wrestlers parade in ceremonial aprons paid for by supporters. Three major basho are held yearly in Tokyo.

Hoisting his ponderous leg, a wrestler prepares to stamp his foot down hard.

Pre-Battle Ceremony

A bout between high-ranking wrestlers involves more time spent on ritual than on wrestling. Combatants warm up with a series of ceremonial preliminaries—squatting, stamping and clapping. For up to four minutes they posture and scatter purifying salt in the ring, trying as they do so to demoralize their opponents by their menacing or disdainful manner.

Before 10,000 eating and drinking spectators seated on the floor of the arena, two sumotori crouch, ready to lunge at the drop of the referee's signalling fan.

In a violent release of tension after the long build-up, two wrestlers collide at last. It is often only ten seconds or so before one man is down and out.

4

Retreat from Old Ways

How did Edo, "Mouth of the River", the shogun's city, become Tokyo, "The Eastern Capital", the seat of the Emperor? Was not the shogun the real ruler of Japan, and the Emperor little more than a figure-head confined to his palace and garden, sitting in the ancient capital of Kyoto? All true—that is, until the 19th Century when the shogun's power crumbled under the internal stress of economic and social problems and the pressure from without of Western nations. After 1854, when Commodore Perry of the U.S. Navy forced Japan to open some of her ports to international traffic, the shogun's government lost most of its credibility, and a period of radical change began.

The problem of Japan's relations with foreigners and foreign powers was not an altogether new one. In 1549, St. Francis Xavier landed at Kagoshima; during his two-year stay in Japan he successfully laid the basis of a vast missionary movement. By the end of the century his followers had made converts by the hundreds of thousands, including some notable *daimyo* lords. These conversions touched a sensitive point in the Japanese conscience. Could Christians be entirely loyal to the Emperor, or would a new loyalty build up, directed to a distant spiritual leader? Around 1587 the suspicions of Hideyoshi, Ieyasu's predecessor, had grown so strong that he decreed the expulsion of all foreign missionaries. For some years the law was ignored, then in 1597, a group of 26 missionaries and converts were crucified at Nagasaki. Persecution gradually increased until the beginning of the 17th Century when Japanese Christianity ended in tragedy. In 1637, after a Christian-led revolt, some 37,000 men, women and children were massacred at Shimabara on the island of Kyushu. Christianity had been virtually eradicated.

In 1639 Iemitsu, Ieyasu's grandson, closed the country to foreigners and those braving his ban were likely to find themselves in the dreaded Kirishitan Yashiki (Christian prison) of Edo, where the last known inmate, the Sicilian priest John Baptiste Sidotti, died miserably in 1715. The Japanese likewise were forbidden to go abroad. Only a small group of Dutch traders were considered trustworthy enough to be permitted to reside on a tiny island near Nagasaki.

The shoguns took pains to hide Japan from prying foreign eyes, making sure especially that the world learned little about Edo. Even the size of the city was kept secret. The Dutch traders were permitted to send occasional deputations to the shogun, but usually saw nothing more of Edo than the visitors' quarters and the route from there to the palace. Members of one

A nightclub hostess, dramatically clad in white, moves through the darkness of a Tokyo side street on her way to work. Her costume consists of a fine kimono, a richly brocaded obi, or sash, and the traditional tabi socks with high-soled clogs. Her red-lacquered parasol adds a calculated splash of colour.

of these delegations in 1806 described being installed in four back rooms of a guarded house while their Japanese escorts and attendants enjoyed the front, more exposed parts of the residence. Only when the house was destroyed by one of the city's periodic fires were they able to move to an inn. There, such crowds gathered to get a peek at them that the governor of the city forbade the Dutchmen to appear on the inn's balcony.

It was easier to confine the strangers than to control Edo's curiosity about them. They were visited by Japanese physicians and astronomers eager to interrogate them about Western science. A parade of high-ranking Japanese men and women trooped through their rooms to ask questions and paw through their wardrobe trunks, brazenly obliging the Europeans to present them with "gifts" of clothing. The traffic in information was one way. "The princes are always friendly, conversable and unwearied questioners respecting European arts, sciences, customs and manners," wrote one Dutchman, "but they never allude to Japanese policy."

In spite of this tack, Edo continued to remain as ignorant of the outside world as Europe was of Edo. In an interview with the shogun and his court in 1822, Dutch merchants were asked—perhaps with a little malice-aforethought—whether Holland ruled its East Indian colonies or vice versa; and whether Europeans had made any progress towards perfecting an immortality drug. The visitors were compelled repeatedly to put on and take off their coats (the Japanese found buttons, unknown in their country, particularly fascinating), "to walk, to stand still, to dance, to jump, to read Dutch, to paint, to sing and innumerable such other apish tricks" for the shogun's edification.

Out through the palace gates rolls a British-style state coach—one of the Imperial Household's 16—to fetch a new ambassador who will present his credentials to the Emperor. The first such coaches (later duplicated in Tokyo) came from England during the 19th-Century period of Westernization.

But already the power of the shoguns was on the wane. Famine, unrest in the countryside and the growing financial power of the merchant class over the impoverished samurai elite shook the foundation of the ancient order. Then, in the 1850s, the whole of the Tokugawa edifice that had been founded on Ieyasu's genius began to crumble.

Unable to solve its economic problems in isolation, continuously under pressure from the Great Powers to conform to the rules of the international community, Japan was in no position to ignore Commodore Perry when he came with four warships in 1853 with the intention of opening the country to American trade. Even so, every effort was made to keep the Americans away foom Edo itself. Negotiations took place at Vraga, about 30 miles down the bay from the city, and when Perry made plain his determination to sail up for a closer look at Edo, the shogun's emissaries were "in great dismay", according to the expedition's official narrative. Perry was told that the water was too shallow, that the citizens would run riot on seeing foreign ships, that he would endanger the safety of the empire and certainly cost the emissaries their lives. The commodore pressed on, but when he reached Edo a fog stole his view. "The general outline of the city could, however, be made out," said the report, "showing an immense and thickly crowded number of houses and buildings covering a large surface . . . there was every indication of the great size of the town."

Like the Dutch before him, Perry found that the Japanese, who wished him to learn nothing, themselves wanted to know everything. They flocked to demonstrations of the small steam railway and electric telegraph he had brought along to show off Western technology. "When visiting the ships, the mandarins and their attendants were never at rest, but went about peering into every nook and corner, peeping into the muzzles of guns, examining curiously the small arms, handling the ropes, measuring the boats, looking eagerly into the engine room, and watching every move-ment of the engineers and workmen"—all the while making notes and sketches on mulberry bark paper they carried for the purpose.

After Perry, the pressure of foreign interest in Japan was unrestrainable and Edo's isolation could no longer be maintained. By the 1860s, British, French, Russian and Dutch envoys had installed themselves in Edo. But recognizing that the supreme power of the land was vested in the Divine Emperor in Kyoto and not in the shogun, they took pains to have their treaties ratified by him.

Ironically, the government of the shogun had been eroded from within by its own most admirable ideals. For it was the shoguns who had decreed, as the noblest embodiment of the samurai code, the ideal of "the Double Way of Warrior and Scholar". By thus encouraging learning, they were unwittingly inviting historians to consider Japan's past—and to realize that the shoguns were usurpers of a power originally invested in the Emperor. This realization made the restoration of imperial power inevitable. And the axis of that momentous turn of events was to be Edo, seat of the shogun.

By 1860 the situation in Edo was desperate. Assassinations were frequent. There were numerous attempts at internal rebellion. The economy was in collapse. Many of the younger samurai, whose ethics had dominated the political fabric of the land for so long, took up the imperialistic slogan "Revere the Emperor! Drive out the barbarians!"

The first permanent British envoy, Sir Rutherford Alcock, described an encounter with some of these angry, intemperate warriors. Approaching his residence on horseback, he ran into a group of them, each armed with two swords ("about as dangerous and deadly weapons as men can possess") and clearly drunk. "Within fifty yards of my own door, having just overtaken Mr. Heusken [an American diplomat, who was killed 18 months later in a similar incident], one of the men—more intoxicated or more insolent than the rest, and not content with standing in our path—pushed against both horse and rider." Alcock's groom thrust him aside, but the samurai reached for his sword. "Fearing a defenceless servant might be cut down by this drunken bravo," wrote Alcock, "I wheeled my horse round, to protect him by interposing myself. . . . But another of my servants had a revolver and, hearing the officer vow immediate vengeance, presented it, declaring he would shoot the samurai if he drew his sword. But for this, both the groom and myself might very probably have been wounded, if not murdered, by this ruffian, maddened with drink and armed to the teeth." The attitude of the samurai towards foreigners, which frequently resulted in such skirmishes, becomes more understandable when it is noted that Alcock's diplomatic mission had been housed, albeit on the shogun's directions, in one of Edo's most important temples; and that the priests had been forced out in order to make room for the British—probably not an exceptional case in the crowded city.

The shogun himself was young, insecure, vacillating, frail of body and without charisma. In these circumstances the apparently changeless order had come to an end, and the city that had so recently been the most populous on the face of the earth began to decline. From 1862 *daimyo* lords were no longer required to reside part of their time at Edo and to keep elaborate establishments there. Uncertainty and fear drove away thousands of people, until by the mid 1860s the population had dropped to no more than 600,000. Land values tumbled, and grass grew in the streets that had been so proudly trod by the to-and-fro processions of the *daimyo* lords calling at the shogun's castle. Foreign legations found it difficult to secure enough food and were never safe from the assaults of fanatics.

In the winter of 1866-67 both the young shogun and the young Emperor died, and the pressures for radical change, even for revolution, became irresistible. The new shogun wisely judged that he could no longer carry the past with him into the present, and returned the supreme governing power, with which he had been invested, to the new Emperor, a 16-year-old

From Feudal Village to Space-Age City

1456	Nobleman Ota Dokan founds castle of Edo by fortifying site near present-day Imperial Palace
1549	Francis Xavier, first Christian missionary to Japan, sets up Jesuit mission in Kagoshima
1560-1598	Oda Nobunga and Toyotomi Hideyoshi, two great military leaders, together bring about unification of Japan by controlling country's warring factions through military dictatorship
1590	Tokugawa Ieyasu takes over Edo and builds immense stone castle
1597	Beginning of Christian persecutions in reaction to growing missionary presence in Japan
1600	Tokugawa Ieyasu defeats coalition of rivals at battle of Sekigahara and becomes de-facto ruler of Japan
1603	Tokugawa Ieyasu is given title of shogun (military governor) by Emperor, ruling in Kyoto. Edo becomes administrative capital of Japan
1604-1614	Edo castle is enlarged and made more magnificent. City of Edo grows up around it
1627	Kanei Temple is founded on Ueno hills to protect city's north-east approach from evil spirits
1634	Shogun Iemitsu requires all daimyo lords (feudal barons) to return to Edo periodically and to keep their families there as permanent hostages. City increases rapidly in size and splendour
1657	Fire destroys two-thirds of Edo
1660	Construction of Edo's first Kabuki theatre, the Kabuki-za
1688-1704	Genroku Era: cultural heyday of Tokugawa administration under great-grandson of Tokugawa Ieyasu. Art and literature of Edo flourish
1703	Disastrous earthquake and fires kill more than 30,000 people
1707-1708	Eruption of Mount Fuji; Edo covered with ashes

boy named Mutsuhito (who is known today by the name given to his reign: Meiji, which means enlightened rule).

Foreign historians call this transfer of power the Meiji restoration, which implies a return to an established but interrupted mode of living; but the Japanese term for it, *ishin*, much more nearly expresses the spirit of the times and the extraordinary task on which the nation now embarked. The word *ishin* stresses the idea of renovation. The deep and elemental nature of the transformation to be undertaken was expressed by the new Emperor on April 6, 1868, when he urged Japan to abolish "old unworthy customs" and to seek knowledge "among the nations of the world" to promote the welfare of the empire. It must have been a time of hair-raising excitement, of colossal adventure and change.

The Japanese set about the task with admirable fervour and a regrettable lack of discrimination. "To preserve or revere old customs and fashions was regarded with contempt," says an official history of the period; "and so far did the fancy run that some gravely entertained the project of abolishing the Japanese language and substituting English for it." The most apparent, immediate effect was in costume. "In short, the Japanese undertook in the most lighthearted manner possible to dress themselves in clothes such as they had never worn before, and which had been made to fit other people," wrote one observer. "The spectacle looked strange enough to justify the apprehensions of foreign critics who asked whether a nation should adapt itself to systems planned by a motley band of aliens who knew nothing of its characters or customs."

Of greater importance was the transformation of the physical environment by new technology, so marked that it became the symbol of "civilization". Even children were affected. In 1878 the words for one of their ball-bouncing chants ran like this: "Gas-lamps, steam engines, horse-carriages, cameras, telegrams, lightning conductors, newspapers, schools, letter-post, steamboats. . . ."

Meanwhile, a most important decision was being made by the new government. For many reasons, most of them no doubt practical but some —and not the least important ones—purely symbolic, it was felt necessary that the court leave the ancient capital of Kyoto and that the central business of government, the focus of power, be moved to the place from which the shoguns had exercised their rule. This was such an important step that a new name for the city seemed appropriate; Edo would perhaps have reminded everybody too much of what had so recently passed away. Tokyo, the name chosen, in its translation, might strike Westerners as dull —the two ideograms that make it up mean "eastern" and "capital". But the word "eastern" offered solace to the abandoned seat of government at Kyoto. Kyoto, officially renamed Saikyo—Western Capital—could go on thinking of itself as equivalent in importance to the newer "eastern" capital. The ideograms for Tokyo were first of all spoken as *Tokei*, and that pronunciation in fact remained in official use for some time; but the more informal and familiar Tokyo was rapidly adopted by everybody else and eventually supplanted the earlier reading even in official business.

The effect of the move was immediate on the newly designated capital; the population at once began to rise again and land prices to climb (although nobody but a visionary could then have dreamt that, a century later, when Tokyo was once more the most populous city of the world, the price of less than a block in the centre of the city would have ransomed Ieyasu himself). But the development that most struck the imagination of those who witnessed it was not the mass removal of officials and functionaries from offices in one city to similar offices in another, but the preliminary visit paid by the young Emperor to his new capital, in 1868, the year of his restoration. Carried in a heavy palanquin of unpainted pawlonia wood, he travelled in a slow, silent, solemn procession all the way along the Tokaido highway from Kyoto to Tokyo. It is possible to do the same journey today by bullet-train in just over three hours: but in 1868, in a ceremonial progress that had not been witnessed for centuries and struck all who saw it with its strangeness, its beauty and its almost eerie simplicity, it took the Emperor's cortège nearly a month to cover the 300-or-so miles.

The apparently deliberate avoidance of the sumptuous military display that had been so much a ceremonial trademark of noblemen or shoguns seemed to herald a simple, more peaceful era. Actually, life could never again be so simple, particularly in the context of the grimly ominous world outside the borders of Japan to which Japanese eyes were now more and more directed. Strangers on the international scene, they found the Far East—their neighbourhood—in the hands of strangers: India under British rule, the French in Indo-China, the Russians just across the Okhotsk Sea, the Dutch entrenched in a vast archipelagic empire to the south, and China itself threatened with subjugation by a whole coalition of Western powers. Furthermore the United States was beginning to understand its huge strength and show it.

The response of the Japanese was to weld together the extremes of their national style. All the intellectual and emotional forces of Japan were brought into an intimate union with its muscles and sinews, and the result emanating from Tokyo was a determined power of astounding dynamism and enormous potential, both for good and for evil.

In many ways the Meiji era, from 1868 to 1912, reproduced the character of the Victorian age in the West. It was immensely confident, industrious, solid, ceremonially ponderous, expansionist, above all successful. It was an age that demanded great sacrifices from most of its people but reaped great benefits for the country as a whole (in part, it is true, at the expense of the nations with whom the Japanese competed or warred: the Chinese, Russians, Koreans and other foreigners). Such was the spirit of the times,

In the ornamental pond of a Tokyo garden, huge carp—respected in Japan for their legendary courage and determination—compete for food tossed by strollers.

however, that the Japanese did not need to look far to find comforting examples of worse things done for lesser reason by nations that were generally, then, thought to be their betters.

During the Meiji era Tokyo grew large, and rich, and important—and ugly. "Fair to look on is the capital of the Tycoon [shogun]," Alcock had written in the early 1860s, before the city changed so dramatically. "The picture that bursts suddenly upon the traveller is very striking." He admired the beauty of the Imperial Enclosure's parklands riding above the dense mass of houses on a range of hills, its triple moats thronging with wildfowl that, when startled, "rise like a dark cloud from the waters, in immense numbers". He was impressed by the big, wooded estates of the *daimyo* lords, arboreal oases of sheltered serenity cut off from the teeming city with high walls and imposing gates.

The public parts of Edo were equally to his liking. "No squalid misery or accumulations of filth encumber the well-cared-for streets," he wrote, "a strange but pleasant contrast with every other Asiatic land I have visited and not a few European cities." He recounted with pleasure his journeys through streets crowded with pedestrians, bullock carts, palanquins, pedlars carrying wares on their backs, porters with hand barrows; and two-sworded samurai on horseback, their servants on foot trotting tirelessly alongside, past the premises of booksellers, coopers, pawnbrokers, clothiers, department stores (one with a hundred sales clerks), printers, basket-makers, sword-makers and bath houses, from which curious bathers rushed naked to see the foreigner passing by. He found the excitement enhanced at nightfall, when the streets were filled with "gaily painted and figured lanterns flitting to and fro," carried—in accordance with the law—by everyone who was out after dark. "No capital in Europe presents so many striking features of a type altogether peculiar," Alcock declared; "nor upon the whole can any boast of so much beauty in the site and surrounding country."

But with the transmutation of Edo to Tokyo there began at once an infection of large, purely utilitarian buildings; and the city assumed something of the shanty-town look that it has now over much of its area, and that is so permanent a part of its character. The difference was noted as early as 1881 in a guide-book: "A great change has taken place since 1868 in the outward appearance of many parts of the city, which were formerly covered with the *ya-shiki* or mansions of the territorial nobility. Many of these have been pulled down to make room for new official buildings. At the same time the disappearance of the two-sworded men (samurai), the displacement of the palanquin by the *jin-riki-sha*, the adoption of foreign dress . . . and the European style of wearing the hair, now almost universal, have robbed the streets of the picturesque aspect which was formerly so great an attraction to the foreign visitor."

In a city twice destroyed since those days—by earthquake in 1923 and

In a Tokyo teahouse a group of women perform the meditative rituals of the tea ceremony. Developed in the 15th Century by Buddhist priests, the ceremony—deemed an artistic discipline that brings mental peace—is widely taught and practised as one of the Social graces. Above, from top: a guest washes her hands at a well in the teahouse garden; the assembled company bows; the tea is mixed with a bamboo whisk.

by bombing in 1945—few monuments of the Meiji era survive. Yet from prints, paintings and early photographs, it is possible to recapture something of the feel of the new capital almost a century ago: ugliness there certainly was, but some major buildings—foreign legations, hotels and the like—clearly had great charm, uniting as they did a certain colonial naiveté with oriental flourishes of dragon gates or pagoda turrets.

The Emperor Meiji was succeeded in 1912 by his 33-year-old son, whose reign was given the name Taisho. It was a short reign—14 years—and, compared with what had happened in his father's time, uneventful. That is not to say that he achieved little. On the contrary, the essential work of consolidating the developments of the restoration years was ably carried on by the *genro*, the elder statesmen, and the respite from the expansion and experiment that had consumed so much energy in the preceding 40 years now permitted a loosening of disciplines. As a result, the brief Taisho era was marked by a distinctively original literature, a new aesthetic awareness, a flowering of social and political conscience, and the beginnings of public participation—or at least awakened interest—in the affairs of the State, all of which helped forge new links with the West. It was marked, too, by tragedy: the catastrophic earthquake and fires of 1923 effectively brought Taisho's reign to an end. His remaining years were spent in ill health, while his son, the regent, who would one day be known to the world as Hirohito, presided over the gigantic task of reconstructing Japan's capital and other important neighbouring cities.

For this reason little remains to remind us of the Taisho era. There is Tokyo railway station, built in 1912 of red brick on the model of the one in Amsterdam: it survives, no doubt, more because it is a monument of industrial archaeology than because of its real, but unashamedly homely, charm. And there is the Akasaka Detached Palace, bearing ambitious and rather pathetic testimony to the confusions that still beset the cultural aspirations of the Taisho period. The Egyptian Room lies uneasily next to halls directly inspired by *Noh* theatre motifs; marbles extravagantly imported from the seats of Classical European culture are discountenanced by overbearing, massive iron gates. It is, in architectural terms, not exactly a success; nor, evidently, were most of the projects by which architects and planners sought to transform Tokyo from a conglomeration of villages into something like an imperial city during the years after 1904-5, when the resounding defeat of Tsarist Russia's navy at Japanese hands gave the impetus of confidence to ambitions already powerfully stirring. All that was lacking, alas, was genius. The outstanding surviving building of the Taisho period is the memorial shrine to the Emperor Meiji, completed in 1920 but in a timeless Shinto style of unobtrusive simplicity, deriving its grandeur from the vast surrounding park and the feeling, strongly realized by its designers, of Nature harmoniously and sensitively in partnership with the work of man. The Shinto ceremonies conducted here are among the most beautiful and moving visual treasures that Tokyo has to offer.

The new era that began with the Emperor Taisho's death in 1926 was called by the name of Showa, "Luminous Peace". If it cannot, in retrospect, be thought an overwhelmingly appropriate choice for a period in which so much destruction and bloodshed were to be perpetrated, it seemed propitious enough at the beginning. There was more freedom, of a personal and public kind, than had been enjoyed in the whole history of Japan. Liberal ideas were in wide circulation and beginning to be expressed in policies. Prosperity was at last spreading beyond the privileged classes, to which it had been limited for centuries. But the governments that succeeded one another were weak and inefficient, all too easily represented as "spineless" by fanatical nationalists or militarists, all too ineffective in dealing with the economic crises that beset the world in 1929-31, all too unable, when at last they acted, to resist the forces of organized totalitarian politics.

In 1931, the unauthorized attack on Mukden and the occupation of Manchuria by the Japanese army capped a series of transgressions against China that were neither condemned nor disowned by the Tokyo government. And it is from that failure to control the military that historians date the entry of Japanese politics into the *kurai-tanima*, the "dark valley", which led inescapably to the heavy rearmament and the international confrontations that had their outcome in the Pacific carnage of 1941-45. On the way to disaster there was a war with China and, not less significantly, an attempted coup by the army in 1936, in which several government Ministers were assassinated. The coup would certainly have succeeded had the young army officers who engineered it been equal in will to the Emperor, in whose name they claimed to be fighting, but who in fact called them mutineers and ordered that they be crushed. The Emperor could not put an end to the ideas behind the coup or their ultimate realization. The militarist myths of invincibility, of celestial intervention on the side of a people chosen to dominate the world, were only to be exploded by defeat —the defeat that was accepted on the day in August, 1945, when the Emperor once again used his supreme power of command, resting on the traditions of two millennia, to force his generals to surrender to the Western Allies. The price paid was a hard one, in blood, and wealth, and international stature. And the Tokyo I described in my first chapter—the one I had come to know as a postgraduate student—lay in utter ruin.

The flourishing city that now stands on the site of so many other cities may have little remaining of the past. But cities are made not only of stone. There is an immortal continuity in the people of Tokyo that transcends the endings and beginnings of the physical city. Even the name of those who are truly of Tokyo—and they acknowledge only those with three generations or more of Tokyo background—harks back to the earlier city; for such a man is called an *Edokko*, a son of Edo. It is right that he should be, since his character is formed as much by the distant origins of his city as by its modern development. Early Edo was a frontier town, rich in opportunities for the brave, the imaginative, the diligent and the lucky. (It is notable that, as late as 1721, there were still almost two men for every woman in Edo.) Those who made Edo their home were very different people from the citizens of Kyoto—settled, ancient, class-ridden and ceremonious; they needed to be in order to survive in a city filled with ambitious men ready to fight for what they wanted: masterless samurai (the *ronin* of the historical romances), labourers, merchants, poets, robbers, the outcasts of quieter places, the hopeful escapees from the stifling frustration of petrified traditions.

In his character and personality, the typical *Edokko* retains some of the reckless, adventurous and ardent spirit of the men who settled Ieyasu's city. He spends freely, responds to challenges and risks with positive pleasure. He (and equally she) is ambitious, even aggressive, delighting in pungent wit and repartee, possibly a little vulgar in a way that would be deplored in Kyoto but is, if allied to intelligence and talent, applauded in Tokyo. As the French historian Noël Nouët described him, the *Edokko* is "a jovial, bold and cunning fellow, loud-mouthed and always ready to pick a quarrel". But he is a man nevertheless imbued with a marked respect for authority, particularly for the proper and efficient use of that authority, and is quick to detect its misuse. That is no doubt why the word *baka* (literally "idiot" or "fool") has a different meaning in Tokyo than it has in Osaka (the commercial capital) or in Kyoto, the old capital and cultural centre of Japan. An Osaka *baka* is someone no good at making money; a Kyoto *baka* is a mannerless oaf given to solecisms. But a Tokyo *baka* is somebody who cannot "sense the prevailing wind".

Recording the Impact of Change

東京名所之内
新橋ステシヨン
蒸汽車鉄道圖

In the early 1870s, passengers wait for a train in Tokyo's new, Western-style Shimbashi Station. Behind the carriages is another new sight: telegraph wires.

The opening of Japan to foreign influence in the 1850s had its greatest effect in—and on—Tokyo. Political, social and industrial changes that, in Europe, had taken centuries were compressed into a few years. People were, understandably, confused by the new ways; there is even a story that passengers on the first railway (above) followed normal custom and removed their shoes before entering the carriages—only to see their footwear left behind as the train pulled out. Although suspicious of Westerners, the Japanese after centuries of isolation also tingled with curiosity about them. In Tokyo artists and publishers of wood-block prints catered to this appetite for information, selling hundreds of captioned pictures of foreigners and the changes they caused. These prints, as much a form of journalism as art, are now collectors' items.

In Western uniforms, envoys returning from abroad report to the Emperor.

The printmakers probably copied these scenes from foreign publications.

The Rush to Adapt

When the "black ships" (foreign vessels) first arrived in Japan, artists reflecting national attitudes depicted them as dreadful, smoke-belching monsters. Later, accounts brought back by Japanese who went overseas helped calm popular fears of the outside world and whetted public demand for views of foreign cities, which Tokyo's enterprising publishers promptly supplied.

長サ七十五間
船巾二十間
車　六間半
帆挺三本
水ヨリ上ノ出
武丈五尺
石火矢十挺
大筒貳十五挺

Japanese motifs—the pedestal lamp on the deck, the temple-shaped deckhouse—appear in a 19th-Century interpretation of a foreign ship by a Tokyo artist.

An English pair use the inevitable British brolly.

An American father slouches in his ill-fitting suit.

Russians take tea. Chairs were unfamiliar in Japan.

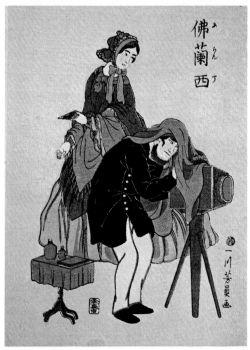

A French couple employ another novelty: a camera.

A Japanese View of the Strangers

During the 1860s, visitors to Tokyo from the provinces rarely returned home without buying wood-block prints to show friends and family what strange creatures foreigners were. Although the artists dutifully portrayed the elongated noses and rounded eyes of their subjects, they often created faces that looked more Oriental than Occidental. Here, captions accompanying each print give a thumbnail sketch of the subject's home country.

This print incorporates two items rarely seen in Tokyo homes until they were made popular by foreigners: a clock and a frame round a picture.

By 1889 the transition from old Japan to a
modern nation was complete, at least in a
superficial sense. Here, a Japanese ensemble
in European dress performs at the Rokumeikan,
a smart club devoted to the enjoyment of
everything Western.

5

Tokyo's Two Worlds

"I warn you—the place is awful, frightening, infernal. A beastly concrete box. Do not think even for a moment about our home in Kyoto as you knew it. That was another Japan. I can hardly imagine a suitable word to describe this place—*shikata ga nai* perhaps—'there is nothing that can be done'. We are on a tiger's back, the tiger is charging through the forest, and we must go on and on. But why should you stay in a hotel? It must be so *sabishii*—'so wretched and lonely'. Come and stay with us again."

Thus, by telephone, on a visit to Tokyo, I received an invitation from an old friend to taste new-style living in one of the many high-rise blocks of flats that have mushroomed all over central Tokyo. The speaker was Mrs. Suenaga who several years ago had taken me into her delightful Kyoto home as a paying guest. Since then she had been widowed and had now moved to the capital so that her son could attend Tokyo University.

I gladly accepted. My hotel was indeed *sabishii*. I much preferred the intimacy of a family home. And frankly I was attracted by sheer curiosity. Each year tens of thousands of Japanese families are uprooted and transplanted into the heart of the most modern and overcrowded metropolis in the world. What is it like, I wondered, to live at the epicentre of an explosion both of population and technology? How strongly does it contrast with the old style of living such as I had experienced in my little house in Town Number Six? And how long can the ancient Japanese traditions and values be maintained in a fast-changing city that is subject to the most rampant modernization?

Mrs. Suenaga described Tokyo as "another world", one totally divorced from the quiet beauty of Kyoto, Japan's ancient capital. And I began to see what she meant from the moment her son Akira arrived to collect me from my hotel. I remembered him as an awkward, pimply youth of 15, impossibly shy, and always dressed in the dreary black uniform with gilded buttons that was typical of Japanese high school students. Now he was 22, a smiling, self-assured young man, casually but fashionably dressed in light pullover and jeans. And he was driving his own car.

"I see you're doing quite well," I said. "In my time Japanese students hardly ever owned cars." He smiled apologetically and explained that he had bought this one very cheaply, second-hand. Sitting beside him in the car was an attractive young woman. "My fiancée, Rumiko," he explained rather nervously. "Oh—but please don't tell my mother about Rumiko. She doesn't know yet." A car and a fiancée! As we sped along the elevated highway I could not help reflecting on the legions of Japanese students I

A monolithic structure of glass and steel dominates a residential Tokyo neighbourhood. Low-level houses are fast disappearing before encroaching high-rise buildings like this one and the others crowding forward in the distance. In the process they are altering the city's way of life as profoundly as its appearance.

had known over the years. I remembered especially my old skiing companion, Haruo. He belonged to a wealthy Tokyo family and in the grim, pre-war years was unusually independent for a student. But even for him the idea of owning a car would have been an extravagant dream almost comparable with the idea of owning a private jet aircraft today. As for a fiancée, well that was beyond imagination then. Some boys whispered of secret visits to one of Tokyo's many red-light districts, but they viewed young girls of their own background as being far too childish and virginal for any kind of free relationship.

We left the highway to drop Rumiko off at her home near Meguro, one of the higher-class residential districts of Tokyo, where the streets are quiet and one sees nothing but row upon row of villas set in immaculate gardens. Then we headed back to the much less salubrious district of Shinagawa, not far from Haneda International Airport. The contrast in living styles could scarcely have been greater, and Mrs. Suenaga's "beastly concrete box" was instantly recognizable—a gigantic block of flats that rose like a Dolomite tower out of a vast jungle of squat houses, temples, workshops, sheds and shacks. Most of the surrounding buildings were wooden with grey-green roofs of tiles or simple tinplate — the kind of flimsy structures that once made up the tinderbox Tokyo that was so often consumed by fire. Now these buildings were not even as big as the name-sign—three colossal characters in Japanese—that topped the flats.

The *manshion*—as such a building is called—was inviting enough in its clinically clean, utilitarian way, and silently a lift whisked us up to the 14th floor where Mrs. Suenaga greeted me with the warmest welcome, pronounced in her delightful Kyoto accent. She had not changed in the slightest. A friendly smile lit her ageless, intelligent face; her diminutive body was clad in a kimono of sober elegance. She might live in a "beastly box" but she still had—and always would have—that supremely refined and subdued taste that the Japanese call *shibui*. She was a teacher of flower arrangement and tea ceremony, and she remained a passionate guardian of everything that is most exquisitely and truly Japanese.

After formal greetings, followed by the inevitable cup of tea, I was shown around the flat. The small kitchen and the lounge-dining room were Western-style. The rest was pure Japanese—or at least, so it appeared. On closer examination, however, I realized that the wooden ceilings and walls, while giving a certain feeling of intimacy, were really no more than plywood a few millimetres thick. Behind them lay cold concrete and steel.

The whole place, spotlessly clean and new, was designed for convenience and efficiency. "I suppose this is the future," said Mrs. Suenaga. "More and more people are living in *manshions* now. One day perhaps Tokyo will be a city entirely of *manshions*. There are fifty families in this box. Can you imagine it? But then think of the space fifty individual houses would take up. And at least the view is lovely from here."

We crowded on to a tiny balcony and looked out on the vast, boiling cauldron of ugliness and splendour that is ultra-modern Tokyo. The giant television tower that is now the city's major landmark stood directly before us and beyond it there was a cluster of skyscrapers half-shrouded in silvery smog.

I was aware of non-stop movement on all sides: yellow taxis, cars, trucks, bicycles, buses, trams, mono-trains—all noisily rushing through the veins and arteries of this staggering cosmopolis. And that was only below us. From above came the continuous thunder of jet airliners streaming in and out of Haneda Airport. The Japanese ideogram for "deaf" shows a dragon sitting upon an ear. At that moment, out on the balcony, I felt that a dozen different dragons were perched on my ears.

Mrs. Suenaga was right. This was indeed "another world"—light years removed from life in Kyoto and her old house in the shadow of the celebrated Daitoku Temple. Her previous home was a modest place—just a two-storey wooden cube with a grey-tiled roof—but it had five or six rooms in pure Japanese style, and it opened out on to an enchanting garden that was subtly designed to have the naturally wild look of one of the many clearings amid the densely wooded hills around Kyoto. There, in sharp contrast to the unrelenting cacophony of Tokyo, the silence at night was broken only by the faintest of sounds—the far-off chanting of a monk in the temple, the chirping of a cricket, or perhaps the splash of a frog landing in the pond and disturbing the resident carp.

Such was Mrs. Suenaga's Kyoto home. Now I was with her and her son in Tokyo. Before retiring on my first night I took a soulless dip in a square plastic basin of pea-soup colour—the water warmed, or course, with the immense efficiency of piped-in gas. How different from that Kyoto bath-

A chic Japanese bride in Western-style wedding gown and her equally fashionable white-suited groom coax a small bridesmaid into line for a photograph on the steps of a Shinto shrine. Like many modern couples, these newly weds were married elsewhere and have come to the shrine to record the moment for posterity in more traditional surroundings.

room with its greenish light in summer—sunshine filtering through the layers of maple leaves outside. But at least the bed was the same—or, to be precise, the *futon*. A true Japanese home does not have a bed. Instead, at night, thick padded quilts called *futon* are pulled out from a recess in the wall and set on the *tatami* mats. The result is a delightfully intimate effect; the entire room can be transformed into a bed in a few minutes.

Like so many people of her generation, Mrs. Suenaga was fighting a gallant, but ultimately losing battle to preserve an exquisite Japanese life-style in the alien soil of central Tokyo. She would always be traditional in outlook, but the new generation of space-city dwellers, as represented by her son, was clearly moving with the relentless tide of change, becoming more and more modernized.

Modernization—and the hazily related term Westernization—are two words frequently bandied about whenever the conflict between the new Tokyo and the old is a topic of conversation. But a Westerner would do well to remember that the words are by no means synonymous here. In essence, modernized signifies being up-to-date in technology, while Westernized implies being influenced generally by the civilization of the West. It is entirely possible for a Japanese to be highly modernized without being Westernized.

But, as we have seen in Tokyo, things are rarely all that they seem. The Japanese businessman, clawing and shoving his way to the office as he joins in the daily animal stampede called the rush-hour, might be considered Westernized. He has certainly abandoned one basic Japanese characteristic: politeness. Yet, follow that same man to his suburban home in the evening and in all probability you find that, once he enters his front door, he changes into more traditional clothes and becomes part of a private world marked by serenity and grace. Such seeming contradictions are the very essence of life in Tokyo today.

One of the most startling developments is the Japanese celebration of Christmas. At first glance this might seem a perfect example of Westernization without modernization. Not so long ago Japan ignored that date. Now the holiday has been taken over from the West. Walk around the shopping districts of Tokyo in mid-December and you'll find streets, shops and hotels decked out with Christmas decorations of all kinds. Now if that is not real Westernization, what is?

But look more closely. The main thing about the holiday—the religious aspect—has been left out entirely. The same might be said, I suppose, about over-commercialized Christmas in many Western countries. In any event the Japanese have developed Christmas into something typically native, a colossal modern *matsuri*. The great Tokyo department stores become modern, magnified versions of the family stalls one sees along the routes to shrines and temples during *matsuri* days all over Japan. As for Santa Claus, he is merely a smiling avatar of Ebisu or Daikoku, two laughing prodigal gods of ancient times. Those idols of good fortune descended from the sky, bringing with them rice cakes and fish; Santa Claus might descend from a jet carrying a bag of electronic toy wonders. But the difference is only in appearances.

Shortly after moving in with the Suenagas, I was invited to a cocktail party. It turned out to be of special interest to me because it allowed me to observe at first-hand a Tokyo family that had been subjected very strongly to Western influence. My hostess was Mrs. Yoneda, mother of Rumiko, the tall, thin girl whom Akira had introduced to me as his fiancée. She spoke near-perfect English, having been educated in France, England and the United States; and everything about her—clothes, jewellery, accessories, gestures, words—revealed an extraordinary chic, something one very rarely encounters among Japanese women attired in Western-style dress.

Mrs. Yoneda's home near Meguro—which I had seen briefly the day Akira had picked me up at my hotel and driven me to his mother's flat— was a solid-looking structure that had escaped the devastation of war. For all the Yoneda family's wealth, it was the kind of anonymous place that makes me think of Thorstein Veblen, the American economist and social scientist who propounded the theory of "conspicuous consumption" to explain why people often buy—and display—things they don't need. Would he have had the same view if he had lived in Japan? I rather doubt it. Until relatively recent times consumption was rarely conspicuous here, a legacy perhaps of two-and-a-half centuries of Tokugawa rule, of the days when samurai were expected to spurn worldly possessions and merchants guarded against ostentation in the knowledge that to parade one's wealth before the feudal lords was to invite severe requisitions.

Of course, the structure of Japanese society has changed radically since then. Look around the luxury shops in Tokyo and you will discover some absurdly extravagant goods: a set of men's underwear in pure vicuna selling at more than $1,000, a rare whisky at $500 a bottle, Chinese and Western antiques costing tens of thousands of dollars. Obviously, some wealthy Japanese must be indulging their expensive tastes. Nevertheless, truly palatial residences in and around Tokyo are still rare. Even Tokyo's prominent citizens and financial tycoons continue to keep a markedly low profile at home; and no Japanese, as far as I know, lives in the stately-home grandeur maintained by some European aristocrats and industrialists and most Middle East oil potentates. It takes a trained eye to read the signs of genuine affluence and distinction here: the size of a garden and the apparent age of its trees, the sight of a well-maintained vintage car in the garage, the presence of servants—especially if they are not mere employees but authentic family retainers.

I could detect a number of these distinguishing features as Mrs. Yoneda ushered me into her home, having first told me not to worry about removing my shoes. "This is a tumbledown barn of the Meiji period," she explained

Standing on the mirror-polished floor of the dazzling, ultra-modern Buddhist Reiyukai Temple in central Tokyo, a lonely couple appear suspended between planes of golden lights (right). The 25-foot-high wooden statue (above), located behind the main altar, stands serene in its strikingly untraditional setting.

gaily. "It must be a hundred years old, something quite prehistoric. But we all love it just like this. I do hope you won't mind."

The "barn" was vast and warm and immensely hospitable. Seemingly priceless Chinese carpets had been spread over the *tatami* mats, and three large rooms had been combined to make a very spacious and irregular living area in Western, open-plan style. There were chairs, tables, sofas, old Japanese chests of drawers, numerous books and flowers. Large patio windows opened on to a garden landscape straight out of an old painted screen—an immaculate, restful bowl of green with ornamental rocks and pine trees gnarled with age. Such a successful marriage of Eastern and Western styles is exceedingly difficult to achieve. The Yonedas had managed it with originality and good taste.

But it was the Western influence on the family itself that interested me most. Above all I was intrigued by the discovery that Akira's girl friend had an elder sister called Nori and that the two girls appeared to have been brought up in totally opposite ways. Rumiko was slouched in an armchair, discussing Inner Energy and Relaxation Response with some slightly effeminate-looking Japanese boys squatting at her feet. She had recently been to New York for training as a professional interior designer, and had taken up completely Western dress, speech, manners, gestures. In striking contrast, Nori was dressed in a kimono, sitting upright on a sofa, and giggling over a magazine with some other girls. In her appearance, movements and speech she was entirely Japanese.

Someone handed round a bowl of tangerines. Nori delicately peeled all the white rind from each slice, then daintily sucked out the juice before depositing the empty skin on a saucer. Rumiko squashed whole slices into her mouth and managed to gobble down two tangerines before her sister was halfway through her first.

Towards the end of the party, Rumiko subtly steered me into a corner for a private chat. Her face was slightly red, perhaps the effect of a second or third aperitif, but she had the situation very much under control and deftly manoeuvred our conversation to her own ends—from modern art to modern youth, and from youth in general to Akira in particular. As she talked, I admired her elegance—all silk and pearls outside and pre-stressed steel somewhere deep inside. The combination was really quite intimidating.

"You have known Akira a long time, I believe." I nodded, and she took another sip of her drink before coming to her real point. "Oh Akira, he's such a dear boy. I simply adore him. But he's a puppy, you see. The other day he introduced me to you as his fiancée. I wish he wouldn't do that! I have told him again and again, but it has little effect. Now, you are rather like a father or an uncle, I hear. So please tell him he is quite mistaken. Of course, he's such a lovable boy. But I am not his fiancée in the least."

Here was a young Japanese lady of an entirely new breed, and her words were quite revolutionary when one remembered all the tragic romances of

Japanese legend that so often portray young women as helpless, ill-fated creatures without the faintest control over their own destinies.

I left the party bewildered, and when I got back to town, the present seemed to hem me in more than ever. But then I came to the triangular area of parkland dotted with bushes and trees and a few stone monuments directly under the balcony of Mrs. Suenga's *manshion*. I had barely taken note of this place before, except for an unusually old-looking, wooden building at the far base of the triangle. Now I was amazed to find that the whole area had been transformed into a festival garden lavishly decorated with lanterns and plastic sprays of maple leaves. The dilapidated old building, similarly festooned, bore a name-sign: "Temple of the Great Sutra", and the Buddhist priests and parish followers were squatted on mats within. Outside, the crowd was multiplying, and stalls offering sweets, toys, souvenirs and religious trinkets were being set up all along the unused side-street that once, in Tokugawa days, had formed part of the ancient Tokaido trunk road between Edo and Kyoto.

High above, on the roofs of tall buildings, brilliant neon lights proclaimed a variety of products: Coca-cola, Mazda Cars, Kenwood Stereo, Nippon Ham, Pirelli Tyres. But down here, by lantern-light, was an enchanting setting for the kind of religious village fair that might have been staged centuries ago in Edo. Children in those bright-coloured summer kimonos called *yukata* ran around with ice-cream cones clutched in their hands like trophies; elderly couples came alive with chatter as they strolled through a scene from their youth; pious people lit incense sticks in front of tall stone monuments and chanted prayers aloud to a drum-beat accompaniment. One monument bore the inscription, "Glory to the Lotus Scripture of the Wonderful Law", suggesting to me that the temple belonged to the zealous Nichiren sect of Buddhism. I made inquiries and discovered that the triangular area, seemingly so insignificant by day, was well-known by the name *Suzu-ga-Mori*, "The Wood of the Bell", a place of unusual historical importance.

The dragon sounds of roaring traffic no longer overwhelmed this landscaped oasis of high-rise Tokyo. Instead, the night air was now filled with the brisk lively beat of drums and the gay music of flutes and tinkling cymbals. It heralded the approach of an extraordinary procession made up of some 25 separate groups of young men, all dressed in blue summer *yukata* with straw sandals on their feet and white towels wrapped as turbans round their heads. These men carried aloft six-foot-high models of wooden pagodas that were brightly lit, inside and out, by dozens of electric bulbs and shaded by umbrellas of wires entwined with paper flowers. Each group was preceded by a band of drummers, flutists and cymbalists, and each band in turn was preceded by two or three muscular men; with great elegance, strength and skill, they rhythmically raised and lowered a long pole crowned by a heavy ornament (*matoi*) that they kept constantly revolving so that its many pendants flew out in a flashing, eye-catching swirl of shiny metal and coloured tassels.

As each group passed by, I was attracted by small, delightful watercolours illuminated inside the pagodas and showing scenes from the life of the 13th-Century dissident Buddhist monk who is known to his followers as Saint Nichiren. "Well, how do you like our *Oeshiki?*" an old man asked. Then he went on to explain that the feast called *Oeshiki* celebrated Saint Nichiren's death. "When Saint Nichiren left this world, it was mid-winter," he explained, "and yet the cherry trees of Japan blossomed as a sign that a great soul had entered Nirvana. That's why there are so many *mando*— those umbrella-like ornaments with paper flowers that are said to represent 10,000 lanterns. They remind us of a great miracle, a prodigy, the blossoming of cherry trees when all vegetation should be sleeping."

The festival atmosphere grew more and more fervent; positively Dionysian in style, as some groups worked themselves into a shamanic frenzy, swaying to the obsessive percussion of the drums and incessantly repeating the litany: "Glory to the Lotus Scripture of the Wonderful Law." Young people, many of them possibly university students, appeared to be completely intoxicated—but only with religious fervour, since there was certainly no liquor available on this Buddhist occasion.

Each group now passed before the largest stone monument, where the men prayed loudly and burned much incense. Then, with great noise and bustle, they moved on towards the temple. There was just one strictly modern touch; each illuminated *mando*, I noticed, trailed a motor-car battery mounted behind on a rubber-wheeled trolley. At the temple the priests and patrons sat solemnly facing the open door, and as the groups came before them the drum-beating and prayer-reciting rose to a crescendo. The confusion was terrible.

Now, more extravagantly than ever, the *matoi* bearers performed prodigious juggling feats. One of them, splendidly sun-tanned and tightly muscled (he wore only the most minute *fundoshi*—loin cloth) launched into a quite extraordinary and frenzied acrobatic dance. For a moment we were lost in some mythological event out of time. Then eyes wandered upwards to follow some sparks lifted on the wind from overheated incense sticks, and there in the background was present-day reality. No gods or angels or dragons in the sky. There was just one enormous translucent neon sign: Coco-cola.

Next morning, when I spoke to Mrs. Suenaga about the festival, she reacted with obvious disapproval. "Oh, so you were down there—among those madmen!" With her strict Zen and samurai background, she was not at all impressed by the wild antics of "those Nichiren people". In fact, she said, they were "simply disgusting". Her reaction was a further reminder of the complexities of Japanese life. It takes a long time to appreciate that, in Japan, all the many variations in taste, attitudes and beliefs are every bit as

At major Tokyo intersections billboards report electronically computed pollution levels. The leftmost number shows the carbon monoxide (CO) in the air at 10 ppm, or "parts per million". The next gives an average CO reading for the last hour—also 10 ppm. The third indicates that noise in the area has reached 76 "hon"—the Japanese counterpart of decibels.

divisive as those one might encounter in the West, separating Protestant from Catholic, Jew from Gentile, Marxist from Liberal, and so on.

I asked Mrs. Suenaga to tell me more about the so-called "Wood of the Bell" directly below her *manshion*. Immediately she became edgy. Finally she explained: "Well, you see, I have never really liked the idea of that place. In Tokugawa days it was one of the main execution grounds of the city of Edo. And, as you know, those Tokugawa people didn't play around. Death sentences were handed out for all manner of offences. Some criminals had their heads cut off—and that was a relatively quick, clean affair. Others were crucified, left there to suffer a terrible, lingering death. Some were burned alive.

"At first it made me sick to think of all the human torment and horrors that place must have seen. And during the nights I felt afraid. Ghosts? I don't know. It just seemed to me that there was a vague, diffused horror creeping around. But slowly I got used to it, and now I feel only deep compassion for those unhappy people. I tell myself that it was the inscrutable working of *karma*—retribution. Perhaps it is good to live here, after all; a lesson in humility and frailty. By the way, when you were down there, did you see the sign commemorating O-shichi?"

I shook my head. "No!" Mrs. Suenaga exclaimed. "Oh, but you must hear about O-shichi. It is a terrible story, very famous. I have heard it so many times and there are so many different versions. It comes up on the stage, in films, even on television. But I never dreamed that one day I would live next door to the place where ——" Mrs. Suenaga broke off dramatically, then composed herself and began her terrible tale.

I will not tell it as she did—with gestures and sighs—but I will compress it down to its essentials. It happened about 300 years ago, and the story begins with a samurai called Tarobei, who was so sick of the poverty that went with his position he gave up his status and became a greengrocer. Later he lost his home and shop in a fire, and so he went to live temporarily with his brother, the head priest of a temple. He took with him his wife and his daughter, O-shichi, a girl of rare beauty and artistic talent.

In those days the sons of wealthy people were often sent away for a time to live in temples as companions to Buddhist priests, who could never marry and who might otherwise feel too lonely. Such a companion was known as a *kosho*. He gained from the experience in terms of wisdom and manners, and in return the priest was deflected from the lure of courtesans. A *kosho* was usually selected for his good looks and good nature, and the one at the temple in our story was especially handsome and charming. His name was Samon, the son of an important samurai, a personal retainer of the Tokugawa family. And, of course, the inevitable happened. Samon and O-shichi fell madly in love without her parents knowing it.

Eventually O-shichi's father's house was rebuilt and the family returned home. The young lovers continued to exchange letters and gifts, but then

Modern Japan's affluence is epitomized by the lavish use of valuable space in the multi-storeyed entrance hall of the Mitsukoshi department store. The sculpture on the grand staircase is a subtle reassurance to customers. It represents the goddess of sincerity.

their secret was discovered and the romance was forbidden. In those days, the choice of partners for life was strictly a matter for the parents or guardians to decide. O-shichi was heartbroken. She had no hope of seeing Samon again. But one day her family was visited by a man called Kichizo, a stupid, irresponsible rogue who planted a dreadful idea in O-shichi's confused mind. "You wish to see Samon again?" he asked. "Well, consider this—a fire brought you to the temple, another fire might do the same."

The seed took root and grew, until one day, in her despair, O-shichi could resist it no longer. On a cold December night she set fire to her father's house. Everything was dry and brittle. The wind rose and the fire spread. Within a few hours all of Edo was enveloped again in one of those terrible conflagrations known ironically as *Edo-bana* (Edo-flowers). Much of the city was turned to ashes. Thousands were burned alive.

During the great fire, Kichizo was arrested for looting—a particularly despicable offence—and to save his own skin he told the authorities of O-shichi's far greater crime. The distracted girl admitted everything. Yet there was massive sympathy for her. The poor girl was believed to be under age. She was seen as being powerless, cruelly possessed by the dangerous demon-dragon of Love. That was the way in those days—not to paint Love as a sweet, ennobling thing, a subject for romances with troubadours and knights, but as something frightening and destructive. Even the authorities, it seems, felt she was too young to be held responsible. But again the unthinking Kichizo talked too much. He blundered by telling everyone how O-shichi had excelled at calligraphy; she had had samples of her work publicly displayed, he said, when she was only 11 years old. Those samples were dated, and they proved conclusively that the girl was now 17—a legally responsible age. There was no way out. Arson was the greatest of crimes. O-shichi was condemned to the stake. She was dressed in her most beautiful kimono and for three days paraded on horseback through the streets of Edo so that everyone should see her and be warned. Then they brought her to the "Wood of the Bell", tied her to a pillar, and there she was burned to her death.

The day after Mrs. Suenaga told me the story of O-shichi, I explored the triangular park more carefully. And finally I came across a small sign that read: "Here in 1683 O-shichi, the greengrocer's daughter, condemned to death for her folly, was finally burned at the stake." Below the sign I noticed a weather-beaten old stone with a large hole in its centre. It was where the pillar had risen—the post to which O-shichi had been tied in her final agony.

Modernization and Westernization have radically changed the face of Tokyo, but they have not lessened the effect of stories like that of O-shichi on the public imagination or destroyed certain traditional qualities of its citizens. That is why the city can seem as outrageously vulgar as a brothel one moment and yet, at other times—against its historic background— evocative, inspiring, even subtly esoteric.

This was driven home to me at, of all places, the Italian Embassy. There I met a Japanese lady who held me entranced with vivid recollections of her childhood, spent in an ancient Tokyo family of warrior traditions. She was a woman of uncertain age, uncommon beauty and extraordinary charm. She wore a light blue kimono with no jewels except for a precious jade *obidome*—the clip for her wide, brocade sash. And, like so many Japanese women, she had a gift for painting unforgettable pictures of the society in which her people once lived:

"It was a world that seems far distant now—something quite inconceivable. We were brought up with a severity and discipline that would be extraordinary now. In winter, for example, there was no heating. Sound economy perhaps, but the idea driven into our heads suggested that warmth was synonymous with weakness. I still remember the endless dark corridors of our home at night, the smooth wooden planks that felt like ice beneath my *tabi* socks, and the wind whistling around and rattling the window panes.

"An old aunt lived in some remote corner of the great house, and once I paid her a visit in the hope of being given a warm cup of tea or a sweet. Ha! Ha! What an absurd idea! Instead, she gave me a lecture on the three Confucian obligations of all women: 'Obey your father now, your husband when it shall be decided, and your eldest son later on!'

"It fitted the general pattern of our lives. Nearly every minute of our long days was scheduled—lectures, flower arrangement, calligraphy, gymnastics, etiquette, English—and our lean English nanny with a dry Victorian humour always lived up to the sternest Confucian ideas. Somewhere in the background we had parents and grandparents, all greatly beloved but for the most part deadly serious and unbending. I must have been very healthy and strong to survive all the pressures. And yet, when I observe my own sons and daughter now and see all the remarkable freedom they enjoy, I hardly know what to think. Curiously, the great question remains: Are they *truly* happier than we were in our youth?"

Who was this lady who had experienced such sweeping changes in the Japanese way of life? I asked our hostess and she whispered: "Oh, she is Madame So-and-So, née Princess Tokugawa." (Contemporary Japanese observe the legal abolition of titles with deadpan seriousness.) I couldn't have cared less about the lady having been born a princess; what gave me an instant thrill was the name. So here, just across the room, was a direct descendant of the great shogun Tokugawa Ieyasu, who, on that auspicious morning of August 1, 1590, had arrived in the village of Edo to make it his capital and found the city that is now Tokyo.

All at once Japan's medieval past seemed that much more real to me. Suddenly, the two-and-a-half centuries of the Tokugawa rule had become a strikingly personal affair. Forget books, maps, documents, charts; here was a miraculous thread of living flesh and eyes and spirit to bridge the gap.

The meeting gave me a rare chance to break through traditional Japanese reticence and formality, and so I eagerly returned to the lady's side and resumed our conversation, all the while regarding her with new eyes as I shamelessly, and rather absurdly, tried to catch some fleeting and magical suggestion of Ieyasu in her features.

As we talked, I admired the minute, clear-cut features of Ieyasu's descendant, but I found nothing of that great ancestor in her physical aspect. Contemporary likenesses of Ieyasu are rare, and I know of only one that has the ring of unflattering truth. It portrays him as a middle-aged man with unshaven face, dressed in plain, brown monkish garb with a humble and rather ugly cap on his head. His mouth is small and tightly closed; and he seems to be concentrating on some difficult or unpleasant thought. This man could certainly have proclaimed, "*L'état, c'est moi!*" and yet he appears as the complete antithesis of the Sun King of France. Viewing his stern, grim appearance, one thinks more of a Far Eastern John Calvin ruling over some vast Geneva on the Pacific. Here is a ruler for whom duty is essentially coloured in grey. And certain of his attitudes are promptly suggested: "Tomorrow it will rain . . ." "All men are thieves. . . ." The phrases vary, but the viewpoint remains the same: never expect too much of anybody or anything. Prudence, circumspection, tactical pessimism, a certain stinginess—all these, plus an extraordinary capacity for planning, on a scale beyond the wildest dreams of ordinary men, must have contributed to the complex make-up of Ieyasu.

We broke off our discussion to join other guests who were filtering out of the embassy to stroll around its beautiful, landscaped grounds. This garden, with its large ornamental pond spanned by a bridge and surrounded by ancient and majestic trees, is one of the most distinctive in all Tokyo. It has survived virtually unchanged from the days when this was the residence of an important *daimyo* lord. And, like the "Wood of the Bell" at Mrs. Suenaga's *manshion*, it has a strange history that reveals much about Tokyo's past and throws some light on the remarkable qualities of her people today.

Someone had suggested that we visit a monument on the far side of the garden. So, large electric torches were handed out and our hosts led the way. "Doesn't it make you think of Fellini's *La Dolce Vita?*" one guest remarked. "All of us marching in procession through the ancestral garden." Everyone laughed. But suddenly I felt uncomfortable, and I sensed that the lady descended from Ieyasu had the same awareness of misplaced frivolity. We both knew what lay ahead. We were approaching a stone memorial. It bore an inscription recording that on this precise spot, among the trees, ten of the 47 loyal retainers of lord Asano had committed *seppuku* (ritual disembowelment) in 1703.

Behind that solemn inscription lies a tragedy that, like the story of O-shichi, has captured the Japanese imagination through two-and-a-half

FOSCO MARAINI

Revering an act of fierce loyalty that took place almost 300 years ago, worshippers at Tokyo's Sengakuji Temple (above) burn incense before the tomb of 47 warriors who avenged their master's death knowing they would probably have to commit ritual suicide afterwards. A crest symbolizing the unity of master and servant (above left), marks the spot where some of the warriors killed themselves.

centuries. The story begins in 1700, when lord Asano of Ako, a castle near the present-day city of Kobe, was designated to greet imperial envoys as they arrived from Kyoto at the castle of Edo. Protocol on such an occasion was rigid and complicated; Asano was to be instructed in court procedure, by lord Kira, the government-appointed expert. Unfortunately, however, Kira was a notorious money-grubber and Asano made the fatal error of neglecting to give him the presents he had come to expect in return for his services. After some weeks of vicious innuendo in private, Kira rebuked Asano in public and, during a quarrel that took place later, Asano drew his short sword and wounded Kira, the corrupt master of ceremonies, in the forehead.

At any time or place, "breaking the shogun's peace" was regarded as a serious crime; breaking it in the shogun's castle was a capital offence, a matter for Tokugawa Tsunayoshi, the shogun himself. A judicial council was convened. It condemned Asano to death by *seppuku*. His family and retainers lost all their privileges and were banished, and his castle at Ako was confiscated, together with all its effects.

Vengeance in such circumstances was strictly forbidden by law. Yet samurai concepts of honour demanded it, and in this case Asano had a chief retainer who fully intended to comply with ancient tradition. His name was Oishi Kuranosuke, a samurai of superior valour and unflinching character, who totally accepted the Confucian principle that "a man cannot live under the same sky with the slayer of his father". For such a loyal retainer it was perfectly logical to extend the same principle to "the slayer of his lord and master".

The Tokugawa administrators in Edo, very much alive to the situation, had Oishi and his men kept under constant surveillance. Kira, the chief of protocol, recognized the dangers too and sent out his spies. Two years passed. Most people forgot about the incident. But Oishi never forgot. He was playing a waiting game. An organized attack on Kira's fortress-like *manshion* was impossible for the time being and so, by living the life of a worthless profligate in the pleasure-quarters of Kyoto, he pretended that he had given up all thought of revenge. His followers also laid low, some even deserting their families to go into hiding. Finally their moment came. On a cold, snowy night in December, 1703, Oishi and 46 other loyal retainers of Asano broke into the guarded mansion and eventually killed the *daimyo* Kira. His head was taken to the Sengakuji Temple and laid on the tomb of lord Asano—"to give rest to his spirit". The debt of honour had been paid.

The citizens of Edo, indeed of all Japan, were astounded by this throw-back to purest feudal tradition. After more than a century of peace, most people were enjoying an era of prosperity, pleasure and refinement. They were totally unprepared for such a stern and heroic interpretation of ancient customs. It revived memories of long-discarded traditions, and it evoked widespread sympathy for the loyal retainers of Asano. But the Tokugawa administration could never tolerate law-breaking on such a scale and with such alarming implications. Many influential citizens, possibly including the shogun himself, tried to save the retainers, but reprieve would have entailed a precedent too dangerous to set.

The avengers of Asano—47 men, ranging in age from 17 to 77—were condemned to ritual suicide and divided into four groups for the act of self-execution. One of these groups was handed over to the lord Matsu-daira, whose garden forms the grounds of the Italian Embassy today. It was here that their *seppuku* took place. The ashes of the 47 *ronin* (masterless samurai) rest near by in the garden of the Sengakuji Temple at Takanawa which is now a place of pilgrimage, with their tomb perpetually adorned with flowers and perfumed with incense.

The martyrdom of the Asano *ronin*—47 lives sacrificed for the satisfaction gained by killing one—struck the Japanese heart and imagination to the core. Barely two weeks after their burial, the tragedy was being drama-tized for the theatre, and since then the story has been the subject of innumerable plays, films, songs, novels, prints, paintings and sculptures. The classic 18th-Century drama "Chushingura", which tells the story, lasts at least ten hours when played in its entirety. The tragedy appeals to both the heart and mind of the Japanese because it embodies to perfection the highest standards of that major Confucian virtue: loyalty. It survives as a supreme example also of that quality most highly regarded in Japan: total and absolute dedication to a purpose or cause once it has been freely resolved upon.

Many aspects of modern Tokyo life may seem to contradict this point, may seem to suggest that such extreme loyalty and dedication have become outmoded or forgotten in an age of cynicism and materialism. Donald Keene, in the preface to his translation of the "Chushingura", actually writes by way of apology that "reading the work today we may sometimes feel slightly uncomfortable"; and the "we" undoubtedly applied to Westerners and to young Japanese alike. But I wonder. Do human societies ever fundamentally change?

In reality, the possibility of coming face to face with a 20th-Century incarnation of Oishi is ever present. The conduct of political fanatics confirms that the spirit of Oishi the avenger lives on as a threat of terror, just as other cases of noble dedication and heroic self-sacrifice confirm that his fundamental virtues can still be a constructive force. The only difference today is that such virtues are viewed rather more realistically. When Lieutenant H. Onoda, who had vowed never to surrender to anyone except at the order of his commanding officer, was found on the island of Lubang 29 years after the end of the Second World War, he won massive public sympathy and admiration. But the younger Japanese did not applaud. They saw him not as a loyal hero but as an anachronism, a soldier who had admirable spirit but who, by present-day standards, was lacking good sense.

After viewing the monument to the immortalized 47, we wandered back towards the embassy building. The night air was now filled with sounds that jolted us back into a modern world far removed from those samurai days under the Tokugawa shoguns. In near-by Keio University, members of the student Jazz Club had launched into the beat of a samba. "Not at all bad," said Mrs. So-and-So née Tokugawa. "Quite like professionals. What do you think?" But I was far away—thinking how dramatically life in Tokyo had changed since the days of her ancestor Ieyasu, the founder of it all.

Fantasies in Steel and Concrete

By moonlight the top floors of an office building with a space-age name—Sky Building—suggest an eerie, almost ominous, monument to naked technology.

All but destroyed during the Second World War, Tokyo has been rebuilt in a mixture of styles and ornaments that, at first glance, owe their inspiration more to the rest of the world than they do to Japan. A Westerner expecting the restrained elegance of more traditional architecture—pagoda roofs, paper screens and formally arranged gardens—might well recoil from the surprise assault: a hotel reminiscent of a fairytale castle,

buildings looking like railway carriages or gargantuan concrete nesting boxes, a huge red telephone adorning one roof, an oversized earth-mover on another. To be sure, there is no escaping their presence in the Tokyo skyline, or their effect; they are commanding. But a closer look reveals their special Japanese quality—the ability of their designers to adopt Western forms and infuse them with Japanese imagination.

The fancifully baroque style of this building and its upper-storey window displays are meant to catch the eyes of romantically inclined brides-to-be. The structure houses several shops that specialize in Western wedding attire.

For all its childlike Disneyland charm this turreted castle with television aerial is for adults only. It is actually a "love" hotel—one that caters mainly to couples without luggage who check in for an idle hour or two.

Tokyo's debt to Los Angeles, the city that first exploited monstrous architectural versions of trade specialities, is acknowledged (above) by this gigantic bulldozer on top of Komatsu Limited's building.

In the Meguro district, a 20-foot-high replica of a red coin-box telephone complete with dangling wire assertively proclaims from the rooftop the business of the Tamura Electric Works, makers of telephone equipment.

The Nakagin "capsule building" in Central Tokyo is a tribute to the Japanese talent for miniaturization, as well as a symptom of Tokyo's shortage of living space. Each portholed capsule is a tiny, but complete, one-room flat with bath.

6

Faith and Tradition

You either love Tokyo or you hate it. But even its detractors sense its vitality—it oozes out of the monster like magnetic radiation. You feel it in the sheer physical presence of crowds and traffic on the move, you feel it where men and women work or participate in sport, you breathe it more subtly in the unparalleled range of cultural activities the city offers—a kaleidoscope of exhibitions, concerts, drama, museum shows, folk festivals, symposia, lectures, debates. Tokyo spreads a canvas more wide and diversified than any other city I know. Past and present, East and West mix in startling juxtapositions that stimulate and fertilize the imagination.

Culture here is no preserve of the élite. Wander into a café for a cup of coffee and you may discover that it is crowded with young people who have gone there as much to listen to classical records as to refresh themselves. Visit a bookshop between noon and 2 p.m. (the student leisure hours) and you may have great difficulty reaching bookshelves blocked by boys and girls who are standing there strictly to read, not to buy. I shall never forget my first shopping expedition to Isetan, the multistorey department store in the Shinjuku district. A sign at the main entrance advertised a display on the eighth floor of rare Chinese ceramics and porcelain, and so I went up by lift to take a brief look round. The lift doors opened on to a great lobby which was crowded from wall to wall with people patiently waiting to enter the exhibition rooms.

An exceptional event? Not at all. It is a common occurrence in Tokyo where art exhibitions are not restricted to the many institutions designed for that purpose. All the big department stores, in Ginza, Shinjuku, Ikebukuro and other districts, are renowned for their special exhibits of contemporary and ancient art. By "shopping around", one is liable to find displays ranging from 14th-Century Buddhist paintings to the works of Modigliani or Francis Bacon, from Ainu handworks to Byzantine manuscripts, from Benin bronzes to Moghul miniatures.

Tokyo provides for virtually every cultural taste and interest. Theatres offer not only traditional *Noh* and *Kabuki* and *Bunraku* (puppet) plays, but ballet and drama from the historic to the avant-garde. Concert halls present the greatest orchestras and soloists from countries East and West. One can attend lectures on the most specialized of subjects ("Flower Symbolism on Late 17th-Century Sword Scabbards") as well as on the most general ("Our Place in the Universe"). There are also debates held by every conceivable study group, from amateur astrologists to Zoroastrians; and facilities for learning about the ancient martial arts, Chinese calligraphy,

In Tokyo's Ueno Park a monumental Buddha in front of a temple seems to muse on a simple offering of chrysanthemums—for centuries, Japan's national flower. The 208-acre park was opened to the public in 1878, and is now the site of numerous museums, shrines and temples.

flower arrangement, miniature tree growing, Zen landscape gardening, the tea or incense ceremony, and so on ad infinitum.

Tokyo has more secondhand bookshops than any other city in the world. One of my favourite outings is to Jimbo-cho in the Kanda district, where more than 300 bookstores, scattered along one main street and its alleyways, offer an unbelievable range of works. And this again reflects the inborn curiosity of the Japanese, their inclination to search for knowledge from all sources and adopt it and modify it for their own purposes.

Yet culture is never mere fodder for the highbrow in this city. Here the very word *bunka* (culture) has a vaguely numinous aura about it. The great majority of the people love *bunka*, respect it, pursue it, believe in it— sometimes, admittedly, to the point of turning a relatively unimportant interest into a mania or a ridiculous fad.

Listening to the voice of rebellious youth—and Tokyo, with more than a hundred universities and colleges, has a greater number of students than any other city in the world—one might easily get a different impression. Young people here are essentially geared to the 20th Century and therefore inclined to dismiss culture in its more traditional forms as irrelevant "bunkum *bunka*". I remember, especially, one evening I spent in debate with a group of radical-minded students. My host was a long-haired youth who had a room in a flimsy, two-storey wooden *geshuku* (student lodgings) in the heart of Hongo, close by a number of major universities; for hours we squatted on *tatami* mats and discussed almost every controversial subject imaginable.

Like students everywhere, they all had their passionate ideas for changing the world and making it a better place. Our host set the pace and the tone with scathing criticisms of aspects of Japanese life that he judged to be outdated. He began by attacking *kanji*, the ideograms of Japanese writing imported from China some 15 centuries ago ("They isolate us from the rest of the world. There are too many walls already dividing humanity so it's criminal to add another one—the *kanji* curtain—around our culture.") It was an arguable point of view, but it soon became apparent that he was fiercely opposed to virtually all the traditional symbols of Japanese culture ("Cherry blossom? I detest that paragon of decadent aestheticism. *Matsuri* festivals? All sheepish mummery to keep the people's face down in the sod.") Anything slightly exotic or old-fashioned was irksome to him. He dreamed vaguely of some kind of spotless, clinical and scientifically regimented Utopia to match the technological wonders of Tokyo—The Space City. Is this young man's dream a vision of Tokyo as it will be a generation from now: the nerve-centre of a utilitarian society dedicated exclusively to materialism and to modernism? I think not. The opposite side of Tokyo's absolute modernism is its cultural heritage. Young radicals may choose to decry it; nevertheless, it is deep-rooted and still very much alive and strong.

Under paper lanterns that will be lit at nightfall, customers swarm an open-air sale of second-hand books. Many of the browsers are students at the several universities that share the neighbourhood with hundreds of bookshops.

Although rival claims are made for Kyoto, Tokyo can fairly argue that it is the cultural capital of Japan by virtue of its enormous concentration of museums, galleries, libraries and educational establishments (almost one-third of the country's colleges and universities), many of which lie in three northern districts—Hongo, Kanda and Ueno. Here, more than anywhere else, is every kind of facility for study and research and experiment. Kanda is renowned for its colleges and bookstores. Ueno has more cultural attractions than any other district of the city; its park alone contains a multiplicity of temples and institutions, including the National Museum, National Science Museum, National Museum of Western Art, the Metropolitan Festival Hall, the Art Gallery, Ueno Library and Ueno Zoo.

Ultimately it was astrological considerations that caused the northern districts to emerge as the centre of Tokyo's intellectual and cultural life. According to an old Japanese tradition, still partly alive, the north-east is regarded as the most inauspicious part of the compass; it is called *kimon* (the Demon's Gate), a passage through which malevolent forces enter and are likely to assail human beings. In the old days settlements were therefore spiritually protected on their north-east side by the presence of a temple and shrine. To the north-east of Edo castle rise the hills of Ueno, and it was there, in 1626, that the shogun Iemitsu had the imposing Kan-ei Buddhist temple built—a saintly shield against all forces of evil. Soon other temples and shrines followed to form a defensive arc on the city's northern side. On a lesser scale, temples also sprang up in the south, so that ultimately Edo was surrounded by an "incense screen"—a ring of spiritual fortresses designed to ward off demons and goblins and ghosts.

With the concentration of temples in the north-east, there came in the 17th Century a great influx of Buddhist monks and acolytes; the shoguns encouraged Confucian schools to develop along independent lines, and it was natural for teachers and students to settle near their Buddhist predecessors. Hayashi Razan, the Confucian tutor to Ieyasu, had long before built up Japan's largest private library at his residence in Ueno; now it developed into a college of liberal arts. By the mid-18th Century there were some 800 teachers and 40,000 students in the area of Ueno, Hongo and Kanda. It was only natural that universities, museums and libraries should join them there.

Curiously, it is within this northern region of Tokyo, so predominantly Buddhist in background, that one now confronts the city's most notable monuments to Christianity: the Nikolai-do—a huge Greek Orthodox cathedral erected in 1884 by the Russian Father Nicolai; and St. Mary's Catholic cathedral, designed in 1949 by Kenzo Tange, the celebrated architect of Tokyo's Olympic Stadium. The two buildings make a distinctive contribution to the Tokyo skyline, but they certainly do not blend in with the overall scene—an appropriate clash perhaps, symbolizing how fundamentally alien are Western religions in Japan.

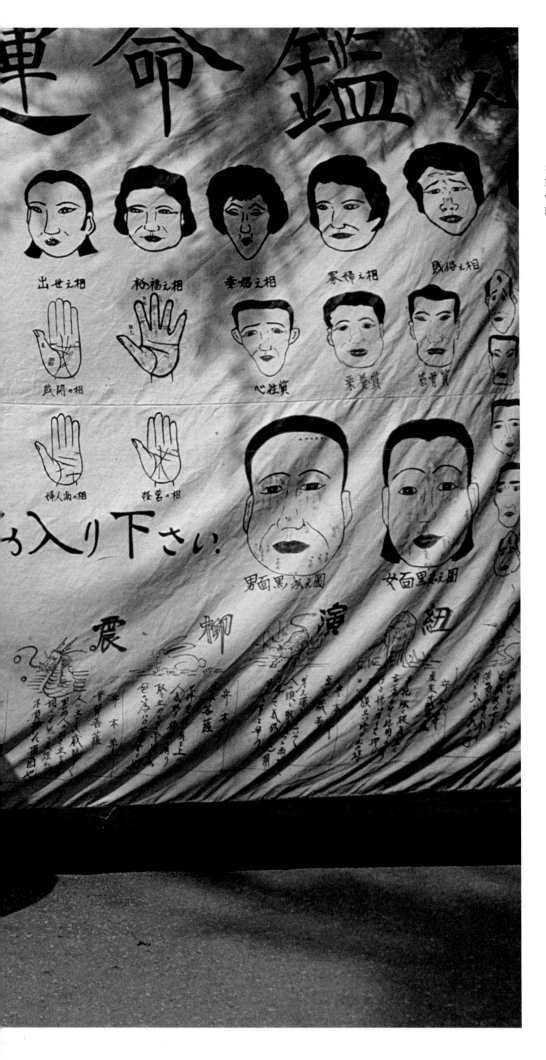

Satchels on backs, two schoolboys fit their hands to the advertisement of a fortune-teller who claims to read the future by scrutinizing his clients' faces as well as their palms.

To gain an introduction to the true nature of Tokyo's spiritual heritage, one cannot do better than travel further north to the hills of Ueno. Ancient prints and paintings show these hills covered by an imposing array of temples—a bright vermilion mass contrast.ng beautifully with the greenery of woods, gardens and orchards. Ueno was outside the city boundaries then, an enchanting place favoured by young lovers and families taking picnics in the country. Today much of that tranquil past survives in 208 acres of parkland that make up the largest of Tokyo's public parks Amid the undergrowth there, one can still discover the occasional stone pillar whose inscription recalls names or events of centuries ago. There, also, one can see the historic, five-tiered wooden pagoda in the precincts of the Toshogu Shrine, built in 1639 and dedicated to the Tokugawa shogun Ieyasu. Miraculously, it has remained undamaged by earthquake or fire, untouched by even one of the three million and more incendiary bombs dropped on Tokyo in 1945. Ironically, the greatest threat to the pagoda came in the 19th Century when some reckless reformers proposed to sell "the old pile of junk" as firewood. Now that "junk" happens to represent a rare example of 17th-Century religious architecture.

On my last outing to Ueno Park I was accompanied by my young friend Akira, Mrs. Suenaga's son. We travelled by underground—the only efficient means of urban transport in Tokyo—and began our walk in the park with a visit to the Tokyo National Museum. There we joined a large crowd meandering through a very important exhibition of *Kamakura* (12th-Century to 14th-Century) sculpture. Ranged around us was a most breath-taking collection of Buddhist images—some majestic, some serene, some tortured, some terrifying. Many were familiar to me from my travels through Japan; but seeing them together in one place, like some magical assembly of gods, was a new and strangely disturbing experience.

Suddenly I was distracted by a gentle nudge from Akira. "Look!" he whispered. "Look over there!" I looked, and across the gallery I saw a diminutive and wizened *obasan* (grandmother) stooped in silent prayer before a gilded wooden image of Buddha. The old lady, neatly attired in steel-grey kimono and spotless *tabi* foot-mittens, seemed completely oblivious to the passing parade. It was a moving sight and, as Akira's reaction indicated, a quite exceptional one; a reminder of how Buddhism in modern Japan has much more to do with culture than with religion. So often today one hears Buddhist monks and priests lamenting the lack of true religious feelings in Japan. "Young and old come in great crowds to our temples. They know everything about iconography, and about cere-monies and their historical background. But they are motivated by *bunka*, not by religion."

Leaving the museum, we began to descend a steep path cutting through trees and bushes. Above us, on the left, rose the small Kiyomizu temple, an authentic 17th-Century relic, painted red and looking at close quarters more like an inviting old barn. Smoke was rising behind the temple. "*Kaji!*" Akira shouted. "Fire! Fire!" And we hurried up the hill to see what was happening. There was indeed a fire, but it was a man-made one and fully under control.

A small group of people, mostly women and girls, were gathered around a courtyard where a priest and his servant were burning dozens of battered dolls in a large iron brazier. Kiyomizu temples, of which there are many, are dedicated to the Bodhisattva Kannon, goddess of mercy. A Bodhisattva, so Buddhists believe, is a celestial being, who has obtained supreme illumination but has postponed the full enjoyment of Nirvana to help all other creatures to reach enlightenment and grace. The Kannon shrine at Ueno is reputed to favour the female sex in particular. At the temple a sterile wife could offer a doll along with her prayers for a successful pregnancy; or a mother could present a doll that belonged to a child who had met an untimely death. On this occasion, pious little girls were also using the open-air crematorium to dispense decently with beloved dolls that were worn out with age.

According to Japanese folk tradition, a doll is no mere plaything but an object treated with so much human tenderness and affection over the years that it comes to harbour the seed of the soul. Therefore, a doll is not simply to be thrown away in a rubbish bin; it is better to dispose of it with proper respect. In some parts of Japan old dolls are still floated downriver or out on the ebbing tide. More often they are destroyed by the surest means of purification: fire.

It was rather touching to see such a simple and ancient ceremony being played out in the heart of Ueno Park. Blue smoke curled into the sky; one thought of incense and how this same scene must have been enacted in precisely the same manner centuries ago. But finally the smoke reached our nostrils and the link with long-past tradition was sadly shattered. The "incense" was the horrid stink of roasting plastic.

Such discordant notes, bringing one back sharply into the 20th Century, are liable to be struck at almost every turn in this park. No part of Tokyo is so rich in both modern attractions and in curious survivals of the past. Continuing down to the park's southernmost point, we could now see Shinobazu Pond, a shallow stretch of water half-filled with lotus plants and artificially created in the shape of Lake Biwa, Japan's largest freshwater lake. On the shore were the contemporary buildings of Tokyo's Aquarium, which is connected to the main zoological gardens by a 328-yard monorail line; and just across the water, linked by three bridges, was an island with a Shinto shrine dedicated to Benten, the only female in a strange group of archaic deities known as "the Seven Gods of Good Fortune". She represents art, music and eloquence and is often depicted playing the Japanese lute.

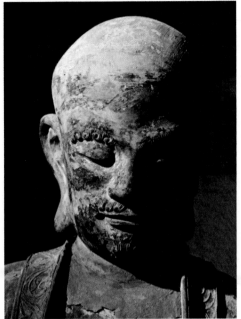

A disciple of Buddha meditates with eyes closed.

A third eye demonstrates a Rakan's vigilance.

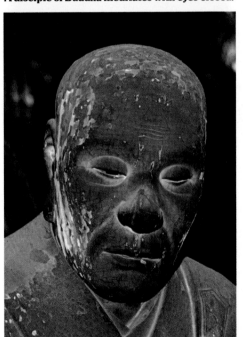

Wisdom and weariness characterize this Rakan.

Huge ears may indicate attentiveness to Buddha.

A Host of Divinities

Images of gods and other venerated beings —wrought in wood, stone and metal—are so plentiful in Tokyo's numerous temples and shrines that they almost form a population of their own. Not all were born in fantasy; some, of the 500 *Rakan*, disciples of Buddha, four of which appear above, have a historical basis. Whether the features of the innumerable deities are grotesque or realistically human, to their worshippers most seem sympathetic and approachable—none more so than Jizo (right), who is the benevolent and much-loved patron saint of children, pregnant women and travellers.

The divinity Jizo, guardian of children, wears a bib given to him by mourning parents who hope he will respond by looking after their lost child in the next world.

Here, so close to new, modern buildings, I discovered a variety of minor shrines consecrated to divine beings with resounding dragonish names and associated with strange fertility cults that had somehow survived from remote agricultural times. Near the edge of the pond stood a venerable stone phallus almost three feet tall, reflected amid dreamy lotus leaves in the water. It looked sad and forlorn, I thought, as if waiting for pious hands to honour it—as in the past—with offerings to ensure fertility in fields long since swallowed up by Tokyo's ever-expanding concrete jungle.

Suddenly, a middle-aged man came into view. He was well-tailored in an expensive grey-flannel suit and looked every inch the successful business executive. To my great surprise, he approached a diminutive shrine standing alongside the phallus and proceeded to bow his head and join his hands in prayer. Was he worshipping at this temple of fertility to seek increased productivity in his factory? Or to increase or regain potency?

Akira glanced at me with an expression of amused superiority. "All this is just silly superstition, ignorant foolishness," he said. "This Shinto fertility business! Are you really interested in such nonsense?"

I answered that I was indeed extremely interested. "Look around you, Akira, and what do you see? Near by we have Benten and her shrine, signs of ancient fertility cults, names of dragons. And all around, over there, we have a skyline of towering concrete buildings, plastered with neon signs and television antennae. Again the two faces of Japan. And they are as consequent to one another as the steps of a rigorous syllogism. Think of industry as a vast neo-fertility spewing out man-made fruits, and suddenly the picture becomes clearer, takes on a degree of logic. Primordial Japan is the proper key to the modern wonder. Pre-history explains future shocks. Fertility cults define the worship of Gross National Product. Village superstition grows into the propellant behind a world power."

The survival of a world of half-forgotten archaic beliefs tells us much about the spiritual development of the Japanese, but for any real appreciation of Tokyo and its people one must be also aware of the profound influences of Buddhism and Confucianism on the country as a whole.

First, we must go back to the mid-6th Century when Buddhism reached Japan from Korea after a thousand-year migration from India. Initially, it was opposed because it might enrage Japan's mythical gods; later, from 594 onwards, it was an officially sponsored religion. In accepting Buddhism, the Japanese did not discard their aboriginal cults of nature, fertility and life, or the *kami* gods, with their picturesque and fantastic myths. The confrontation with the new faith of Buddha merely prompted them to put a name to the ancestral religion that had long been a part of their everyday lives. They called it Shindo or Shinto—"the Way of the Gods".

In time the two religions became complementary, flourishing in fruitful co-existence. The Japanese tendency to include rather than exclude, to reach a compromise rather than assert a divisive distinction, had won the

In the grounds of a temple on the outskirts of Tokyo, a group of yamabushi—Buddhist ascetics who spend their weekends and spare time on religious pilgrimages throughout Japan—prepare to participate in their periodic fire ritual. Some members blow on traditional triton shells to announce the start of the ceremony, in which a number of yamabushi will walk unscathed over live coals. They believe that the ritual enhances their spiritual power.

day. One theory ascribed to the great 9th-Century Buddhist sage Kobo-Daishi, brings the two religions together very ingeniously by explaining that Shinto gods are to be considered avatars—manifestations of celestial Buddhas. But in any event, there never was a serious theological clash. Quite simply, Shinto is connected with worldly interests—with birth and marriage, agriculture and fertility, and the affairs of the State. Buddhism, on the other hand, looks far beyond, over vast spiritual horizons, thus encompassing death and decay, the anguish and mystery of life.

As a result, the religion practised through the centuries by most Japanese is a composite faith, with strands of Buddhism and Shinto inter-mingled at every imaginable level. In a famous 13th-Century diary kept by Lady Nijo, a Kyoto noblewoman, we discover that it was a perfectly normal part of her life to copy out pages and pages of holy Buddhist scriptures as an act of piety, and to offer the fruits of her labour to Shinto shrines.

After more than half a millennium, this blending of religions has barely changed. It is still quite normal for a Tokyo family to present a new-born child at the local Shinto shrine and to solemnize a funeral with a Buddhist ceremony. It has even been known for a man to be employed in the dual capacity of Buddhist priest and Shinto shrine attendant. A few years ago a census was taken of the number of registered Buddhists in Japan, and separately a rough count was made of Shinto followers. The combined total far exceeded the total population of the country—a clear indication that many Japanese do not see one religion excluding the other.

Yet the two religions are quite distinct in their separate influences on Tokyo life. Shinto, for example, always put a great emphasis on cleanliness, purity and simplicity. It was responsible for the bath coming to be regarded as an essential of life, cleansing the spirit as well as the body. It inspired architecture of a most unostentatious style, distinguished by clean-cut lines and plain materials. In contrast, Buddhism gives Japan its metaphysical dimensions—all the subtleties of nostalgia and allusion, the richness of symbolism, the awareness of impermanence, the courage to confront suffering and death with stoicism.

It was Chinese Buddhist masters who introduced the Japanese to refinements in flower arrangement and landscape gardening. More importantly, Korean scribes were responsible for introducing the Chinese system of writing to Japan in the 5th Century. But from China, too, there later came something quite distinct from Buddhism—the philosophies of Confucius which were to pervade the whole of the Japanese political system especially from the 17th Century onwards.

When Ieyasu established the Tokugawa dynasty, he shrewdly supported both Shinto and Buddhism. Around Edo, he ordered to be rebuilt the ancient temples of both religions that had fallen into disrepair; he contributed funds and granted them government protection. But while he encouraged the religions, it was the teachings of Confucius that this wily and wordly genius recognized as the solid ideological base for building stable Japanese society and government. "If we cannot clarify the principle of human relations," he said, "disorders will never cease." His choice was momentous. Its effects are visible everywhere around us in modern Tokyo, and I shall explain how.

While Buddhism and Shinto served religious needs, Confucianism flourished essentially as a philosophy—a profoundly humanistic and humanizing one that provided a rational system of ethics whereby men could live in a well-ordered society. Man was not considered in the abstract but in concrete terms pertaining to five relationships: Emperor-subject, father-son, man-wife, elder brother-younger brother, friend-friend. The rules governing the relationships may have been trite formulae for an organized society, but they embodied essentials easily understood by the masses. They encouraged reverence for ancestors, loyalty to authority, and respect for the family head, with traditions of obedience and duty extending well up the social scale. They preached the importance of patience, responsibility and courtesy.

Today, anyone wishing to see shades of old-style Confucian conduct should go to the platform of Tokyo Station from which the bullet trains leave. Check first with a Japanese calendar, however, and ensure that it is a *taian* (a Vastly Safe and Fully Assured Day), much favoured for weddings. At least five of these days occur in every month; and on a *taian*, one is likely to see family groups assembled at the station to wave newly weds off on their honeymoon. They gather in parties of 20 or 30 people, all dressed in their very best outfits—mothers and aunts in black ceremonial kimonos embroidered with flowers, the bride usually in Western dress with a hat and a veil, the bridesmaids in long-sleeved kimonos and looking as fresh as a field of lilies in spring. Every detail is supremely *comme il faut*. But this is pure pageantry. Once the bell rings to announce the train's imminent departure, the solemn rituals begin, with the important art of bowing displayed in all its refinements and subtleties. The slightest variations in movement indicate individual relationships and personal status: that deep, majestic bow of the senior member of the family to an important guest; that condescending bow of the prominent businessman aware of his own superiority; the vigorous bows of athletic, military or nationalistic types; the dive-bows of self-conscious virgins; the awkward, half-disguised bows of nervous young men who clearly hate to be there and cannot wait to get away to a party in their favourite discotheque.

Confucianism may now seem defunct in so far as it no longer has a place in formal education and many young people are ignorant of its precise teachings. In reality, however, it permeates society at every level and influences behaviour in a myriad subtle ways. That influence extends far beyond the superficial social courtesies—so much bowing and exchanging of gifts and name cards; it cuts deep into the very core of the Japanese way (and hence the Tokyo way) of life. People with centuries of Confucian tradition in their blood have passed through the equivalent of a national course in good citizenship. They possess a near-inborn sense of order and responsibility; their respect for authority gives corporate power to groups and ensures national cohesion.

The practical advantages of such tradition in developing a highly organized industrial state are obvious, and nowhere do they show up more strikingly than in Tokyo. Indeed, the advantages are so enormous and of such fundamental importance that one is prompted to wonder whether this incredible vortex of humanity could have survived in its present state without the stabilizing influence of that ancient philosophy. The density of the population is staggering, the congestion during the rush-hours has to be seen to be believed. At the central Shinjuku Station they actually employ men exclusively for the purpose of pushing passengers into trains and getting the doors to close.

How can so many millions of people tolerate such compressed living conditions, such a frenetic tempo to their everyday routine? Any explanation has to recognize a partial debt to Confucius; his concept of *Rei*—a word involving etiquette, manners and rites but without any precise Western equivalent—has spread down through the centuries to provide a kind of social lubricant: it enables a seething mass of humanity to rub shoulder-to-shoulder without creating so much friction that the machinery of city life breaks down altogether. Many foreigners complain that there is far too much hypocrisy behind the outward show of civility and all the social ritual. This is probably true in Tokyo. Nevertheless, it works. The traditional patterns of social behaviour really do help to prevent this schizophrenic city from having a complete nervous breakdown.

If further evidence of the vital influence of Confucianism is required, one need look no further than Tokyo's quite extraordinary record for law and order. This city has all the recognized ingredients for an appalling crime situation: severe overcrowding, an acute housing shortage, a wealth of materialistic temptations, a booming night-life industry that offers many highly permissive attractions. Yet the crime rate—in terms of murders, robberies and muggings—is astonishingly low. Compared with New York, Tokyo has no law-and-order problem. Again, this cannot be explained without acknowledging a debt to Confucian-based respect for authority and the tradition whereby one man's crime brings shame not only on himself but his entire family and the community in which he lives.

In contrast, there is less evidence of Buddhist influence on contemporary Tokyo living. It has certainly had the most profound influence on Japanese art, taste, criticism, language, poetry, drama, sculpture, architecture, pottery, garden design, flower arrangement—indeed, all interests involving aestheticism—and continues to do so. But, in suggesting that material acquisitions are of little value on this earth, almost to the point of propagating poverty as a virtue, its high spiritual values are at odds with life in the competitive atmosphere of Tokyo today.

In this respect, Shinto is infinitely more relevant. It has become fashionable among Japanese intellectuals to play down the influence of Shinto; some connect it with militarism and disasters, others mock it as an excuse for frivolous *matsuri*, designed to amuse lovers of folklore like myself. But, as we shall explore further in the next chapter, while Confucianism has provided modern industry with an invaluable legacy in terms of self-discipline, loyalty and respect for authority, it is Shinto—emphasizing the good things of this life rather than the hereafter—that has permitted all the razzle-dazzle.

There are occasions in Tokyo when all the diverse cultural strands come together at once. For me, the most memorable episode was, of all things, a funeral—the wake of a very dear friend who died suddenly in the midst of life, at the peak of his powers and personal magnetism. I had known Masa Moroi since before the war; he had even visited me in Italy. I had only recently been to see him at the nightclub he owned, and I was shocked by the news of his death. The funeral ceremony, I learned, was to take place at the Hilton Hotel.

Arriving at the Hilton with me were mourners by the dozen—a cosmopolitan crowd that reflected Masa's innumerable friendships, the variety of his interests, experiences, activities. Moreover, the Japanese among them seemed to be an extraordinarily mixed group, at least as far as class divisions go. There were what I took to be gardeners and jowled company presidents as well as lean, suave aristocrats.

We were ushered into a ballroom that had been lavishly decorated with flowers. Somewhere unseen a pop orchestra was playing a tune with a particularly pressing rhythm. On one side of the room an altar had been set up and—as is normal at Japanese funerals—a massive photograph

The mitsutomoe symbol—three comma-like shapes in a circle, each pursuing the tail of the next—is seen everywhere in Tokyo. The six examples shown here appear on a brass portable shrine carried at Shinto festivals (top row, left and bottom row, left), on drums (top row, right and bottom row, right), as a fabric pattern (middle row, left), and on a wood panel at a Shinto shrine (middle row, right). The mitsutomoe may once have signified the three treasures of Buddhism—the Buddha, the law and the laity—but the precise theological meaning of the symbol has been blurred over centuries of popular use.

of Masa had been placed on top. Taken in summer sunshine, it showed him in sports shirt, radiating all his extraordinary charm. However, the altar instead of bearing the usual candles, incense, sacred Buddhist objects and images was covered with a spectacular display of flowers, fruits, vegetables, fish, wines and *saké*. There was something so wonderfully clear, pure, bright, vigorous and pagan about it all—the inimitable spirit of Shinto—in the midst of a Buddhist rite.

Mrs. Moroi, an exotic beauty in her forties, greeted us dressed in a mauve, Western-style gown. Standing beside her were Masa's son and daughter, both in their early twenties. Mrs. Moroi distributed beaming smiles with a total lack of self-consciousness. That smiles should accompany death is an old point of Japanese—or, at least of *samurai*—etiquette. "Masa wished it like this", Myriam (that was her Western name) said. She invited us "to have a good time and enjoy ourselves and be gay, drink, dance, sing". She reminded us that "his spirit will rejoice if you rejoice". We moved around, slightly dazzled by it all. "Moroi est mort, vive Moroi!" said a French voice.

I joined a queue winding up to the altar and there paid my respects in front of Masa's photograph, with a brief *o-jigi* bow. I found myself deeply moved—not only because I had so recently seen Masa, and because so many memories of the past came crowding up inside me, but because this farewell was so typical of him. I stood motionless for a moment in front of the picture: "*Ciao,*" I said to myself. "Goodbye, Masa."

I mingled with the guests, and all of us, it turned out, had been similarly moved. When the last person had paid his respects, we were invited to sit down for the feast. We took our places at tables that had been gorgeously set. Food was abundant, conversation rich, lively, polyglot, spicy. We drank wines from as far away as Bordeaux and as close as Kofu, at the foot of Mount Fuji. Soon the ecumenical wake was in full swing. The curtains concealing a stage at one end of the room were drawn aside and, before we could get over our surprise, a ballet ensemble—some 20 dancers, actors and singers—had launched into an entertainment. The performers, some of whom were Westerners, danced, acted, sang with tremendous gusto and skill. Flesh was gloriously exposed and propelled us into an orbit of secret warmth. If the message Masa intended to convey to us was *ex morte viva*, he could hardly have been more successful.

During a brief interval, an Englishman sitting next to me said that he had once attended a similar funeral in California; but, he added, "It came off very poorly: we were all embarrassed." He wondered why this one should seem so natural. Yes, why?

That was to set us thinking. The two wakes reflected, we decided, two entirely different concepts of death. In our society, with its Judaeo-Christian base, it is impossible to cavort with death on such familiar, confident, intimate terms. In the Christian mind, at least, death is a gate leading to final judgment, and woe to those who take it lightly. Death seals and congeals the past, defines the future forever. But in the Buddhist view of things, death is a trail to be confronted many times along the path of psychic migration; the way may be hard for all, but the final goal—Buddhahood and deliverance—shines like the sun, inviting mankind onward. In the Shinto view, death leads to the world of the *kami*, where gods and mortals mingle and interfuse. Both faiths permit death to be taken with a smile, an inevitable link in the chain of generation-destruction-generation.

And so, Masa's funeral became his *jisei*, his deathbed poem—written not in words, but in people, music and dance. We were his ideograms, his thoughts, languors, dreams, hopes. When the show was over, the curtains were closed. After the applause ended, there ensued a few moments of silence and darkness. Then the curtains parted again. There, bathed in green light, stood a young couple—he in dinner jacket, she in a long white gown, holding a bunch of flowers. I recognized the boy immediately; he was Masa's son. Mrs. Moroi addressed us from a microphone at her table: "Dear friends, I am performing my duty and following Masa's last wishes. This is Sada, our son, whom most of you know well, and next to him stands Yuri—his fiancée from this moment on. Their marriage will take place in the near future. May they be happy forever!" She stopped abruptly, tears in her eyes. We all clapped.

Yuri was delightfully petite, coy in her movements, accustomed, it would seem, to floodlights and publicity. She was, I was told, a singer. "Yuri, Yuri, Yuri," her young friends began to chant. "Sing something for us. Come on, Yuri. Yu-ri, Yu-ri, Yu-ri." Yuri nodded. A microphone was brought to her. She clasped it in her hands. Now there was total silence. She opened her mouth. Out of her parted lips, very finely, very richly, with total incongruity, came a familiar song—Gounod's *Ave Maria.*

A Crowded Calendar of Celebrations

Flames lick through a funeral pyre of dolls at the Buddhist Doll Festival of September 25, where toys grown old are respectfully despatched by burning.

Some 250 local festivals—combining piety, folk beliefs and simple neighbourhood merrymaking—are celebrated during the course of each year at Tokyo's many different shrines and temples. While some of the ceremonies have remained unchanged for centuries, others are 20th-Century revivals of lapsed customs—such as the Doll Festival illustrated above—that have nevertheless established themselves as firmly as the rest. The ceremonies derive from Japan's two chief religions: Shinto and Buddhism. Shinto the indigenous religion of Japan is essentially a worship of the divine element in Nature, and has been practised since before recorded history; Buddhism, with its emphasis on personal and spiritual progress, was imported from mainland Asia in A.D. 552. The two faiths thrive today without conflict: many Japanese believe in both.

Dancers in stiff courtly dress perform on a stage spread with green brocade.

Court Music with Distant Echoes

To celebrate Culture Day on November 3, scholars from the imperial music school in the palace grounds give a three-day performance of age-old court-style music and dancing at the Meiji Shrine. Such spectacles—played out in lavish costumes—have survived within the imperial household almost unchanged from their 8th-Century origins to the present.

A musician emphasizes a dramatic moment in the dance with a stroke on his drum. Other ancient instruments used include smaller drums, flutes and gong.

Stripped to show traditional tattooing, a young man twirls a standard.

Homage to a Buddhist Saint

One of Tokyo's most tumultuous festivals is *Oeshiki*. Held in October, it commemorates the death of Nichiren, a Buddhist evangelist. In the evening, worshippers converge on the Ikegami Hommonji Temple where, legend says, Nichiren died in 1282. Local groups are led by standard-bearers who delight the crowds with their skill in manipulating heavy, decorated poles.

First arrivals halt at a great bronze incense burner to offer a preliminary prayer. As other groups follow them the streets become filled with jostling crowds.

Exhaustion shows on the faces of the young men labouring under the massive supports of a portable shrine. Bystanders often refresh them with rice wine.

Day-Long Procession for the Gods

Most Shinto shrines in Tokyo hold local festivals to honour the *kami* or gods. On such occasions portable shrines, called *mikoshi*, are brought out of storage. After a ceremony in which the priest reads a ritual invitation to the gods calling on them to come down and partake of food and entertainment, the heavy, sumptuously decorated shrines are hoisted on to the shoulders of volunteers and are carried by relays through the cheerful crowds.

Reserve carriers, some already stripped for action, wait to take their turn with a shrine. Many strong men are needed, since the processions often last for hours.

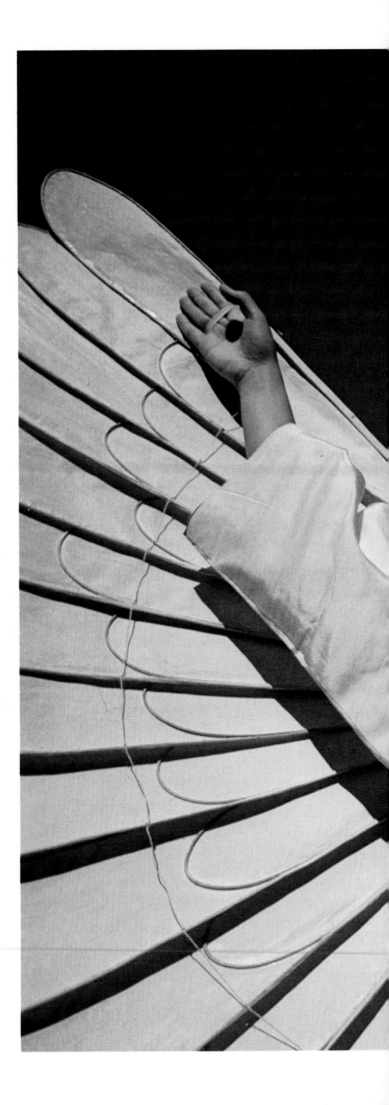

Four of the eight "herons"—all danced by girls—circle with spread wings.

An Ancient Ceremony Revived

Originating in the dim past, more than a thousand years ago, the *Shirasagi-no Mai*—the White Heron's dance—is performed annually at the Asakusa Kannon Temple in the heart of Tokyo. Thought to have started in Kyoto as a ritual to expel disease, it lapsed in the 17th Century, but was re-created in Tokyo in 1968 to celebrate the centenary of the Meiji Restoration.

A dancer pauses, framed by her pinions. The dance, now more an entertainment than a liturgy, begins with a parade of costumed warriors and musicians.

7

The Great God Success

It is Christmas in Tokyo. From the bustling Ginza to the modest back-street arcades, shops and stores resound like immense music boxes with the piped-out melodies of "Jingle Bells", "White Christmas", "Rudolph the Red-Nosed Reindeer" and "Silent Night". The streets are festooned with pine trees, silvery leaves, artificial snow, gigantic cherubs, cardboard reindeer, sugary madonnas and glittering icicles of plastic. Santa Claus is ubiquitous—represented in paintings and sculptures and neon-lit images, and by men in long white beards or glamour girls in provocative skirts.

The great pagan *matsuri* that the Japanese call *Kurisumasu* is in full swing. The sun has passed its solstitial nadir, life is on the upsurge again, abundance and fertility—and industrial productivity—are all being celebrated. Tidal waves of humanity flood through the man-made canyons of Tokyo's towering blocks of glass and concrete and steel and, since every worker has received a lump-sum bonus (one of two given a year, which together can add up to as much as four months' wages) *Kurisumasu* launches a mass spending spree. It also happens to coincide with *o-seibo*, the season for exchanging gifts with friends and business contacts.

Nowhere in Tokyo is this ritual enacted on a more stylish and spectacular scale than at Mitsukoshi. This is the cathedral of department stores and the world's oldest, founded in the 17th Century.

It is an eight-storeyed treasure-house of Arabian Nights splendour, with its own theatre and a Shinto temple on the roof garden. In its breathtaking grandeur, colour and range, it equals and in some instances surpasses the best aspects of Macy's or Printemps or Harrods, and it makes the eyes boggle from the moment one steps through the entrance into the main hall and beholds a multicoloured statue that represents the Goddess of Sincerity (page 108). The idea of personifying "sincerity" is a relatively recent innovation, but the underlying ethical ideal is an ancient one that runs like a golden thread through centuries of Japanese tradition, literature and language. The word *makoto* (sincerity) comes up constantly in the evaluation of one's own or other people's conduct, motives and thought.

The presence of the Goddess of Sincerity, smiling down from on high in Mitsukoshi, somehow reassures the customer that everyone is getting a square deal. It also reminds the Westerner that he is moving in a spiritual world structurally different from his own, one that allows rays of mysticism to penetrate subtly into areas that, in his home country, would be considered exclusively secular. These great department stores—and Tokyo has more than two dozen of them—are, in many ways, "Temples of Things",

A stack of unfinished cameras await their casings in Tokyo's Nikon factory, which each year produces about half a million of these complex and costly packages of precision workmanship. Almost half the world's annual outlay on cameras goes to the 11 Japanese camera companies based in Tokyo.

and never do they seem more so than during the Christmas/New Year season. Within them one senses a reverence for material objects that transcends mere commercial interests. Certainly, the loving care with which sale items are displayed, handled and wrapped has elements that go beyond the purely utilitarian exchange of goods for money. Just as tea drinking has blossomed into the "tea ceremony", so buying and selling goods often resembles a "thing ceremony".

Try, for example, to carry away a purchase without all its ritualistic wrappings and the salesgirl will look at you with utter horror, an expression betraying the unspoken thought that here is an uncouth barbarian if ever there was one. Even in the holiday stampede I have always met with the same obsessive attention to detail. I remember especially going to Mitsukoshi late on Christmas Eve and buying a teapot in the crockery and lacquer-ware department. People were milling all around, but the smiling salesgirl remained perfectly relaxed and unhurried as she neatly fitted the pot into a wooden box and wrapped it immaculately. And when I specified that I intended to give it away, she produced special wrapping paper with red and white decorations, and made up a finished parcel, with a traditional strip of *noshi* (paper simulating dried abalone) attached rather as someone in the West might add a sprig of holly. Finally she handed it to me with more smiles and best wishes for the coming year. The goddess of the store would have approved; the salesgirl exuded sincerity with every word and expression.

Christmas is a relatively new and short-lived *matsuri*, and a Japanese festival that is held in far greater regard very quickly pushes it aside. On the morning of December 26 all the tinselled trappings of Christmas are taken down to clear the way for decorations in celebration of *O-Shogatsu*, the New Year. It is the most important of all seasonal events: a public holiday. Every house is decked inside and out in traditional style.

New Year decorations vary according to local custom, but three things are standard everywhere: pine tree, bamboo and plum tree twigs. The evergreen pine branches signify strength and longevity; the bamboo symbolizes vitality, because it grows fast, and resilience because it bends with the wind. The plum, as the earliest tree to blossom, sometimes even in winter snow, besides heralding spring, represents courage and endurance. Under the old lunar calendar, when New Year fell in February, the first plum blossoms were eagerly gathered to crown all decorative displays. Unfortunately, although hothouses can work miracles, plum blossoms are hardly available in late December and so bare twigs or artificial blossom must suffice to complete the triad.

Pine, bamboo and plum blossoms can be seen all over Tokyo at the turn of the year—outside homes, offices, shops, stores, banks, stations, garages. But the one decoration that is most evocative of the season is the so-called gate pine—bamboo and pine branches affixed to a base made of

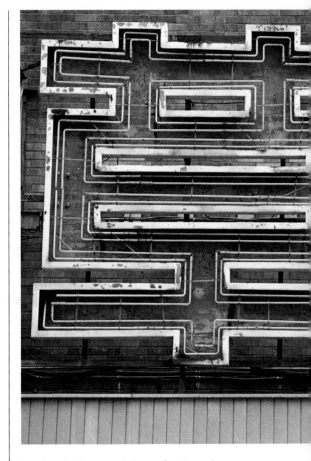

Flanked by the neon tubing of a sign, a busy employee takes advantage of an open window to catch a breath of fresh air while at the same time talking on the telephone.

straw ropes and placed in doorways. From a straw rope, suspended overhead to welcome the god of the New Year into the home, hang strips of neatly folded white paper. The rope is known as a *shimenawa*, a sacred twine associated with one of the most famous of all Japanese myths. According to this legend, Amaterasu, the Sun Goddess, hid in a mountain cave because she had been offended by the violence of her brother, Susa-no-o. The world was plunged into darkness and a crowd of gods tried to persuade Amaterasu to come out of hiding. All their efforts failed until, finally, Ame-no-Uzume, Goddess of Mirth, sang and danced wildly in front of the cave. The assembled gods made so much noise that Amaterasu peeked out of the darkness. Light flooded back into the world and immediately a straw rope was strung across the entrance to the grotto to prevent the sun from disappearing inside again.

The spiritual force behind the New Year celebrations is powerful and real. On the last day of December it is time in Tokyo, as throughout Japan, to complete preparations for starting life anew, and the commercial madness of the previous weeks is forgotten. Houses are cleaned, old clothes discarded, outstanding bills paid. Then, as midnight draws near, the temple bells ring out 108 times, a reminder, among other things, of the number of evils in Buddhist lore that plague the world of men. As the last vibration fades away, a New Year has dawned and Tokyo citizens, dressed in best suits and finest kimonos, flock in their tens of thousands to shrines and temples to pray for good fortune and success.

Bonfires illuminate the shrines, lanterns light the temples and, from midnight until late in the evening on New Year's Day, they will all be crowded. Many Japanese stay up to see the first sunrise of the year. Afterwards they pay special attention to the first bath of the year and have a traditional breakfast that always includes *zoni*, a soup with a piece of rice-cake in it, and cold foods delicately laid out in lacquer boxes. Finally, on January 6, the celebrations end with the burning of decorations, an event conducted with particular ceremony at the Torigoe Shrine in Tokyo's Asakusa district. Everyone walks around the great bonfire beating the ground with bamboo sticks and shouting, "*Dondon yaki* (Burn fiercely)!" A household may save just one small branch of pine from the fires and preserve it in a vase in remembrance. When it withers and dies, the New Year has fully established itself; February has almost arrived.

Pine, bamboo and other New Year decorations symbolize many different things, but the fundamental idea behind them is always the same. They all constitute a forceful reminder of the basic spiritual factor in Japanese life: Shinto vitalism. Western religions stress spiritual values to such an extent that it would appear strange, if not downright blasphemous, to pray openly in church for worldly success and abundance, and to develop an entire symbolism to support those aims. Not so in Japan. In Christian terms, one might almost describe Japanese shrines as versions of Lourdes designed for broken businessmen, for paralysed finances, for unhealthy bank accounts. In the same way, "Work is good" and "Success is worthy" are dicta of Shinto religion just as much as "God is Good" is a fundamental maxim of Western religion. Life is uncomplicated here by any sense of need to equate those dicta with Christian or even Buddhist ethical values.

Herein lies the tap-root of Japan's miraculous economic growth and Tokyo's post-war resurgence, the chief explanation of how a country without great mineral wealth of its own has become the world's third largest exporter. But many factors, besides its peoples' traditional obsession with work, favoured Japan's spectacular advance after its comparatively late industrial revolution. There was the existence since the 18th Century of large cities—Edo/Tokyo being the largest—inhabited by a well-developed bourgeoisie and governed by a competent bureaucracy; the advantages of widespread literacy, of efficient communications via an imposing system of highways, and of standardization of language, weights and measures, and administration over the entire country.

One other important factor is often overlooked: the presence in Japanese society of many first-rate artisans who formed a regular class of citizens trained from childhood to achieve standards of the highest professional excellence. Their accomplishments suggest why Japanese workers of today have managed to excel so soon in so many branches of industry requiring precision and patience. Entirely new technical skills may be needed to produce cameras, radios, television sets and scientific instruments, but they also involve basic requirements in terms of natural aptitudes and an eye for details that have flourished in Japan down through the ages.

The European manager of an Olivetti plant in Tokyo has repeatedly expressed to me his amazement at the high degree of precision in the work of the humblest Japanese labourers: "Technicians are expected to be trained that way, but here everyone seems to have fingers and eyes that can work miracles." I myself cannot help feeling that the extraordinary manual dexterity of the Japanese, plus their uncanny power of visual analysis, is somehow connected with their use of ideographic script. Children still need to learn at least 2,000 *kanji* signs and in so doing they constantly refine their capacity for perception of minute but significant differences. A mere dot can completely change the meaning of a word; entire groups of ideograms may be related by sound although unrelated by form, and vice-versa. To avoid misunderstandings and at the same time read fluently, it is necessary for conditioned reflexes to work furiously and function instantaneously—for the eyes and the brain to operate in unison like high-speed compact computers. Learning to read and write may be an uphill enterprise in Japan for the young, but providentially the mental agility, precision and determination needed to learn *kanji* pay back enormous dividends at the industrial level.

Signs and skyscrapers reveal that the Ginza—by night an

In Tokyo, 35 per cent of the city's labour force is engaged in industrial production. Many Westerners have a preconceived picture of industry being controlled there by mammoth corporations—workers organized in gigantic beehives to make steel, mass-produce cameras, watches, sewing machines, motor cars, plastics, and all kinds of electronic equipment. In fact, large factories and establishments—those with more than 300 employees—represent a small percentage of Japanese industry. The percentage is curiously lower in the capital city where an extraordinary number of smaller family businesses flourish. Among these are four—Yonoya (combs), Domyo (silk kimono cords), Kyukyo-do (incense) and Kammo (sea-food)—that go back to the 17th Century, and a score of others dating from the 18th or early 19th Century when Japan had not yet been opened up to the rest of the world. Moreover, many of the traditional crafts that were threatened with extinction by the industrial revolution are now encouraged by government policies that officially recognize and protect master artisans who are designated "Living National Treasures".

Industrial enterprise, whether in the small workshop or gigantic factory, is typical of Tokyo, something deeply ingrained in the character of the *Edokko*, the true Tokyoite. An *Edokko* likes to start in business on his own, adventurously, perhaps opening a small workshop in his backyard, helped at first by his immediate family and later taking on additional employees who become no less members of his "family". Representative of this old-style citizen of Tokyo is Isao Tanaka, whom I first met shortly after the war through our common interest in photography. He was a man of no formal education; the war had sucked him into its whirlpool too soon and thrown him back too late. But he had natural intelligence and intuition, the sensitivity of an artist, and enough initiative to open a little second-hand camera shop in an alley near the Shimbashi railway station.

In the late 1940s Tanaka-san invited me back to his home, and I was especially pleased to accept because it gave me what was then a rare opportunity to set foot inside a genuine *Shitamachi* home. *Shitamachi* literally means "downtown", but not in the American sense of the word. It refers to that section of the city built on low alluvial plains lying less than 17 feet above sea level, most of which were reclaimed from the sea after 1600. In feudal times, this area, developed along and between the rivers Sumida and Arakawa, was strictly the district of artisans and merchants, who regarded themselves as the true sons of Edo. It was the opposite of *Yamanote* or *Yamate* (the hills), the diluvial upland to the west and north of Edo castle where *daimyo* lords and retainers had their residences. Both sides of the city were proud to be different, and the distinction, with a certain amount of rivalry, survives to this day. Foreign visitors are inevitably channelled into *Yamate* Tokyo, where nearly all of the hotels, and most of the high-class residential districts and cultural institutions are to be found. They rarely see anything of the poorer and

entertainment district—is by day a commercial centre.

uglier *Shitamachi* district. Yet the area is in many ways far more representative of the real city and its people.

Until a few years ago Mr. Tanaka's *Shitamachi* home was a mere wooden box with a green-painted roof under which he lived in cramped conditions with his wife and three children. But recently, when I went back to see him, I found his circumstances greatly changed, so much so that I needed to consult the nearest neighbourhood map to find out exactly where he lived. His old wooden shack had disappeared. In its place stood a new two-storey building of wood and plaster. Outside its large annex I found a sign: "Tanaka Precision Works."

At the front door I was greeted by Mrs. Tanaka, a cordial woman, stout and short, and with a curious knack of gliding about the house as though she were moving on wheels rather than on tiny feet. "Come in with your shoes on," she said cheerfully. Her new home was warm and comfortable, brimful with electrical appliances and television sets; and the living room, where we sat down to tea and cakes, was essentially Western-style. I was now re-introduced to three young men who were small schoolboys when last we met. The eldest boy had graduated from a top-class university and now worked for one of Japan's super-élite electronic companies. "He's definitely on the escalator," said Tanaka-san proudly. "No more worries for him." The second boy was in charge of the family precision works, basically a camera-repair business, while the youngest helped Papa Tanaka in his retail camera shop, now a thriving concern selling the very latest equipment.

I remarked on how far they had progressed since our last meeting. "Yes, it was certainly very different in the old days," said Mrs. Tanaka. "When the shop faltered, we used to repair cameras late into the night. And later, when the precision works was losing money, the shop only just kept our heads above water." The old man grinned. Now snug and secure in his little house in *Shitamachi*, he had a right to feel proud. He had started out as little more than an industrious pauper; now he was a self-made micro-capitalist. Luck, determination and lifelong industry had enabled him to graduate to middle-class status, whereas many others of his kind had finished their days as taxi-drivers or janitors.

In the *Shitamachi* district, there are similar homes alongside modest workshops producing all manner of articles, from pencils and rubber stamps to batteries and bicycle gears and pumps. Some of these family-based enterprises have been inevitably swallowed up by the larger companies which they once supplied. Nevertheless, Tokyo still has many thousands of Mr. Tanakas operating small firms with only a dozen or so employees, and such businesses continue to make an extremely important contribution to the national economy.

The other, more familiar, side of Tokyo industry is the larger-scale *kaisha*. The dictionary defines *kaisha* as a company, corporation, firm or concern, but it is really much more than that. It is a whole way of life.

In Tokyo, fire drills for employees involve more than learning how to escape the premises quickly. Here staff members train with fire extinguishers in front of their office building. The man in the foreground has scored a bullseye, knocking over his target.

Whereas a Western company "engages" an employee, a *kaisha* "envelops" him. The individual gives his *kaisha* a life of devotion in exchange for life-long security. "I help you to function, you help me to flourish" is the unwritten understanding. The system derives from both the feudal *han* (clan) and from the family unit, the *ie* (house). Members of the *ie* (pronounced "eeyeh") were not necessarily blood relations; assimilation and adoption could bind them together as strongly as biological lineage. Similarly, today, even though changing jobs is no longer unheard of, the large Japanese company still fosters a sense of family togetherness. A good employer is expected to have the responsible attitude of a good parent—a kind of "uncle" figure who advises his workers on their personal problems, helps them with their housing arrangements, holiday plans, recreational activities, even perhaps becomes involved in their matrimonial aspirations. In return, the employee gives maximum loyalty and effort, takes the attitude of a good team player who does not wish to let his side down. This group mentality has also played a crucial part in Japan's unparalleled economic growth-rate in modern times.

Mr. Tanaka's eldest son, Teruo, belongs to this world of the *kaisha*. Unlike his father, a low-born *Edokko*, he has followed a cushioned, far more certain path. He has been steered through a good university, taken on by a company that recruits executive trainees exclusively from graduates. Now, as his father says, he is truly "on the escalator". He is what the Japanese, borrowing from the English language, call a "*sarariman*", a salary man, with his wages on a sliding scale strictly geared to the length of his service with his professional "family". He has few worries at present and—barring some quite unexpected disaster—a secure future.

Teruo, a placid, suave and well-dressed man in his early thirties, lives with his wife and young child in a small apartment on the tenth floor of an immense *manshion* not far from Shibuya, a comfortable inner suburb. The letter-and-key boxes at the main entrance to the building bear at least 200 names—ranging from the commonplace Shimizu (Clear Water) and Murata (Village Field) to such an outlandish surname as Domeki (Hundred-Eyed Demon)—and they give one an immediate visual sense of the great conglomeration of people within. This ferro-concrete pagoda reminds me of the Suenagas' apartment block near Shinagawa. However, the apartment itself is not the same. Teruo's rooms, like those of his parents, are filled with electrical appliances: two television sets, a large washing machine, a dishwasher, a refrigerator, a deep-freeze, hi-fi equipment, and a wide assortment of minor labour-saving gadgets.

It seems to me that Teruo's wife, Naomi, has an easy time of it. For years she has taken courses in flower arranging, and several of her elaborate compositions dominate the room—one in the *tokonoma* alcove. Unfortunately, she belongs to the avant-garde Sogetsu school, which cherishes combinations of weirdly shaped vases filled with extravagant flowers and

such objects as purple feathers or tortured fragments of iron. I find it painfully artificial, a homage to garbage rather than to Nature. But then Naomi, I sense, judges me to be hopelessly old-fashioned and out-of-date.

Teruo, who is very modern as well, has taken after his father in only one respect: he is a compulsive photographer. For him, life seems to be wasted if it is not properly and constantly recorded on film. Tanaka-san is adventurous and romantic in his photography; he loves to wander around old temples to take pictures of stone Buddhas or out on to the streets to capture saturnalian crowds revelling in a *matsuri*. In contrast, Teruo is bureaucratic, systematic, ceremonial—and overwhelmingly domestic—in his approach. The resulting output is all carefully filed in a stack of albums.

Volume One of "The Pictorial History of the Junior Tanakas" is devoted to the wedding and to the honeymoon trip to Guam and Hong Kong. Volume Two is about the house they bought for an investment and will soon be entirely their property, purchased by instalments reinforced by company bonuses and family gifts. Teruo explains: "The rent will allow us to put aside money for the children's education."

Volume Three is all about the electronic plant where Teruo is employed, and here I must say his compulsive photography becomes fascinating. It enables him to take me on an armchair tour of the factory that is his modern shrine and castle combined, his very own *kaisha*. It is all here. He has diligently taken his camera to the office, to the workshop, to the company bathroom, to the athletics stadium, to the Buddhist temple near Tokyo where the whole staff passed three days in meditation, with occasional breaks for practising calligraphy and Japanese fencing. We see pictures, too, of Teruo doing his daily *chorei* (morning ceremony)—"In our plant we only do gymnastics; but my cousin, who works for another company, starts his day's work reciting the *kaisha* creed and pledging diligence, honesty and gratitude. They also sing the *kaisha's* anthem there."

At that moment, as Teruo closed the last of his albums, a loose picture fell to the floor. Naomi picked it up hurriedly, but too late. Realizing that I had already glimpsed it, she giggled and showed the photograph openly. "Well, yes," she explained. "Teruo loves to relax sometimes . . . However, I have put a strict limit on it of five thousand yen a month." At last I have found a small crack in the orthodox life of Teuro, the paragon of the good "*sarariman*". I feel relieved. A healthy person needs a few cracks to let out steam, and Teruo's weakness is *pachinko*, the vertical pin-ball game that has become a drug to Japanese of all ages, sexes, classes and incomes. In most amusement halls dozens of these mechanical toys appear in rows, producing the obstreperous din of a factory floor.

Looking around Teruo's gadget-filled apartment it seemed to me quite natural that he should be attracted to this mechanical form of escapism that is so soulless and lacking in imagination. And when I had left his apartment and was travelling by underground across the centre of Tokyo

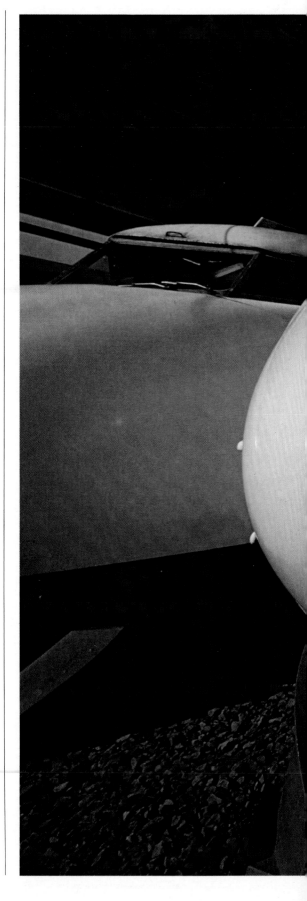

Tokyo's space-age answer to transport problems, these sleek bullet trains cover the 320 miles to Osaka in little more than three hours, reaching 130 m.p.h.

I thought of him again as I looked up at the advertisements that are plastered all over the cars. "Get married with $2,000, trip to Hawaii included," said one sign. "Buy your home by instalments. Generous loans to all with monthly salary: no questions asked!" said another. "Tired? Relax in our turkish baths." "Arrange for an inspiring resting-place for your old parents: book space in the Pine-Hill Spirit-Field Cemetery." So they went, nearly all of them directed at the average "*sarariman*" and his family; and after seeing Teruo at home with his wife and his albums, I appreciated all the more the sound commercial sense the advertisements made.

Everywhere in Tokyo one confronts this kind of "*sarariman*" *bunka* (salary man culture): the never-ending pursuit of middle-class security and status symbols; the new religion of "my home", "my car", "my children's school". In every way, Teruo is a paler and softer human specimen than his father. But then, to be realistic, it is the Teruos—this vast, rather homogeneous, uninteresting and uninspiring mass of commuters— who are largely responsible for keeping the wheels of Japan Inc. turning relentlessly forward, filling and emptying the cornucopia of goods.

Akasaka is one of my favourite districts in Tokyo: a jumble of hills and gardens, of narrow alleys and wide, noisy avenues, an area throbbing with vitality and offering surprises at every turn. Ginza has more shops, Asakusa more folklore, Shinjuku more night life, Hongo and Kanda more learning. But no other part of the city has so much of everything in so compact a space. Here, shacks and palaces collide in delightful contrast. The Hilton hotel towers over the sacred enclosures of *Hie* Shrine where many splendid rituals are held in honour of the god Onamuji and his monkey messengers. The modern Sophia University stands within view of ancient Buddhist temples. The New Otani hotel rises like a futuristic castle on a hill a stone's throw from the Toyokawa Inari Shrine, where the rice god Inari dwells with his faithful messengers, grinning foxes behind scores of red torii gates.

Such contrasts are endless in Akasaka. Foreign diplomatic residences are within walking distance of the most intimate and costly "pleasure houses", places where Tokyo businessmen will discreetly convene, with or without geisha girls (available at $100 an hour and often very much more). Naturally, with so much variety, so many sights, superior restaurants and amusement centres, Akasaka is a popular tourist centre. It is also an excellent area for catching a glimpse of Japanese business life at the top.

I last went there at the invitation of an acquaintance. "Come to my humble shack," Mr. Omura said, "and see some of my Chinese paintings." I chuckled to myself at that description; I was already familiar with these "humble shacks" of Akasaka. True, from the outside, they resemble small wooden pavilions. But it is not unusual to see a business tycoon silently ghosting up to one in his chauffeur-driven Rolls-Royce; and when you consider the astronomical land prices in this district, when you realize that each beam of the pavilion is made of highest-grade wood and that the carefully selected ornamental stones in the garden have probably come from the gorges of Shikoku, or from Taiwan, you begin to understand that these shacks are unpretentious versions of the *daimyo* residence of old Edo.

Mr. Omura can afford Akasaka land prices—just as he affords his fabulous collection of Chinese paintings and his membership of the most exclusive golf club in Tokyo. This is a man who has attained the Elysium of Japanese society—the world of *shacho*, of company chiefs and eminent bureaucrats. He shows all the outward signs: he is well-groomed, well-fed. Being a *shacho* is not in itself a supreme pinnacle of achievement, but being the *shacho* of a large, prestigious company is absolutely everything.

Indeed, when visiting him in his palatial Tokyo office, I experienced the strange sensation of having somehow stepped back through the centuries into a medieval court where one needed to pass by many guards and through many doors before reaching the inner sanctum and coming face to face with one's lord and master. Mr. Omura had provided me in advance with a special card of introduction. Nevertheless, I had to endure a long-drawn-out ritual, being passed from secretary to secretary, ushered into one waiting room after another. Finally, after what seemed an eternity, a door slid open and there was the Great One in his executive suite. He was squatted on a carpet, serenely occupied in painting bamboo leaves!

Mr. Omura seemed completely relaxed. But then he is a man who presents many different faces—sometimes haggard and intense, sometimes silent, thoughtful and rather unnerving, sometimes extrovert, smiling and exuding a certain boyish charm. At all times, however, like every *shacho* of high rank, he wears a charismatic halo and enjoys an advantage that scarcely any president or chairman in the Western world can hope to obtain. Men at his level are virtually the new *daimyo* lords of our age— 20th-Century equivalents of the 16th-Century feudal barons. In those days, great *daimyo* were warrior-chiefs leading their faithful samurai to carve out provinces as their personal, or family, estates. Today they are Captains of Industry, leading their ever-loyal employees in pursuit of a wider world market, a larger slice of Gross National Product. The methods and the aims have changed; the status of the man within the social structure, remains basically the same.

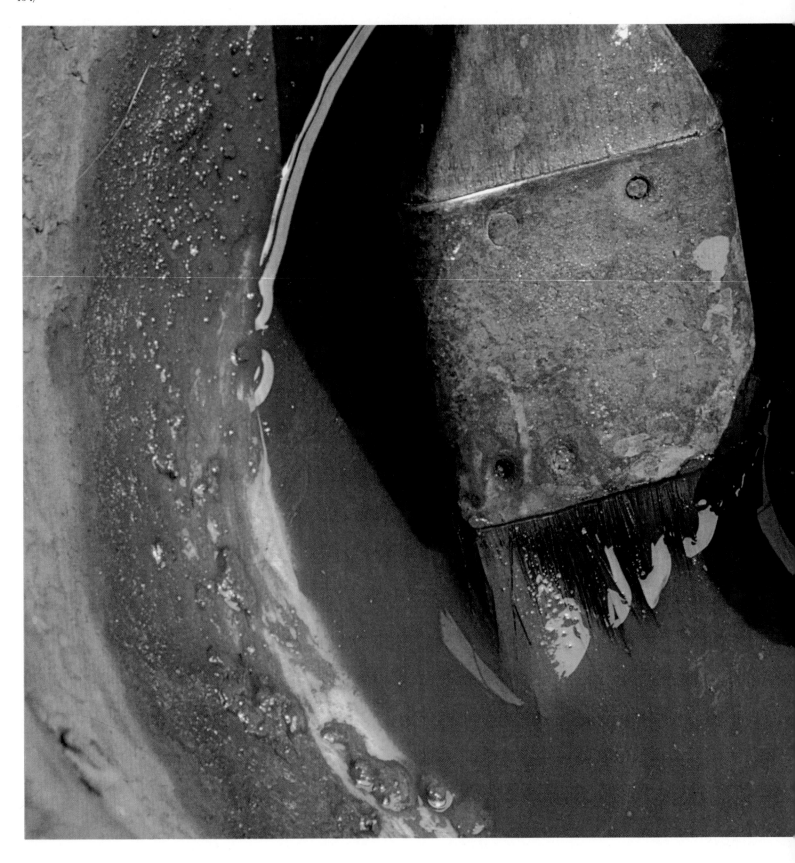

A Heritage of Crafts

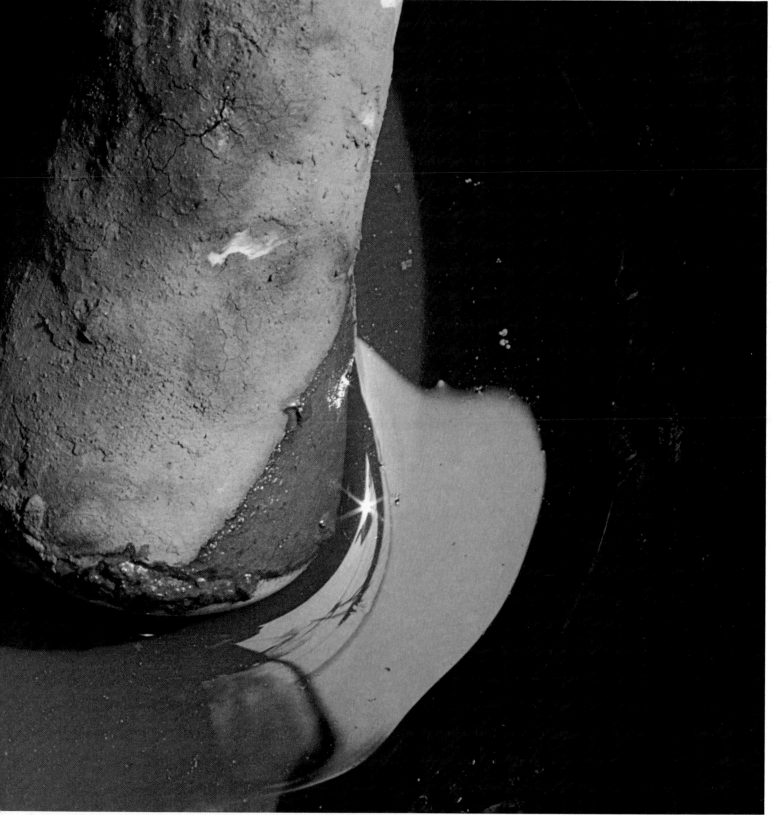

Encrusted brush and pestle in a kite-maker's paint pot form a study in green. Kites of bamboo and paper have been flown in Japan since the 6th Century A.D.

Tokyo is widely held to be the paradigm of the modern industrial city, where computerized production lines spew out with intimidating efficiency the sleek new products of our age. But it is also a city where craftsmen, using time-honoured techniques, still turn out artifacts of simple but impressive beauty. The works of art that they produce range from swords and hand-dyed cloth to items that, in the West, are usually measured as trivia: kites and combs and dolls. Fundamental to their approach is a deep-rooted respect for the old ways—the use of ancient designs, basic tools and natural materials at every stage of their creative efforts. As these skilled, dedicated artisans work at their benches and in their workshops, they are helping to keep alive for future generations an essential and irreplaceable part of Japan's unique cultural heritage.

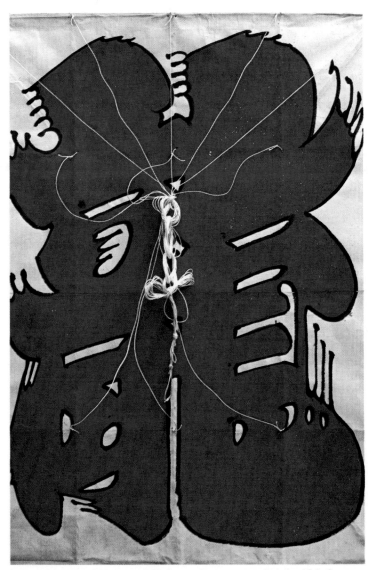

This calligraphic kite is modelled on a design created in the 18th Century.

Kites Tied to the Past

Kites have long been much more than toys to the people of Tokyo. Originally flown as symbolic thank-offerings to the gods, early types bore written characters of good omen. Present-day kites—still made by dedicated masters who have undergone rigorous training—are usually adorned with bold, bright designs of traditional subjects, like the Kabuki actors at right.

Master kite-maker Tako Hashimoto and his wife work in their living-room. Apprenticed until 40, Hashimoto was only then allowed to paint kites on his own.

Designs on moisture-resistant paper stencils like this one are cut by hand.

To fix the dye, strips of cloth are treated with a liquid made from soya-beans.

Delicately Dyed Designs

The methods that Tokyo textile dyers use to produce their traditionally patterned fabrics
have scarcely changed since the 17th Century. First a paper stencil is used to apply a dye-
resistant paste to the fabric, so that when the cloth is immersed in the dye the finely detailed
design remains uncoloured. The dyed cloth is next coated with a fixative and left to dry.
Finally each length is washed to reveal the pattern in white on the richly coloured ground.

A design of pine branches is made up of white stencilled dots. Pine trees, like chrysanthemums (left), are among Japan's most popular decorative motifs.

Hand-made combs prove their maker's infallible eye and steady hand.

Fragrant Combs of Wood

Combs meticulously carved of aged, fragrant wood typify the Japanese delight in simplicity and the use of natural materials. Final polishing of the teeth is done with a special file covered with abrasive leaves. So exacting is the process that one comb may take the man above five hours to complete. He is the 14th generation of his family to produce combs.

Sitting cross-legged on his workshop bench the artisan files the teeth of a comb made from a wedge-shaped block of wood like those in the bundle at his right.

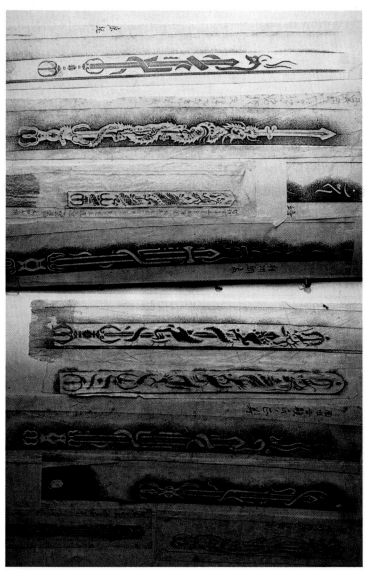

A book of traditional patterns is still used as a guide by a Tokyo swordsmith.

The smith incises a decorative design in the tempered steel of a blade.

Tempered Swords of Honour

Swordsmiths enjoy status above that of all other craftsmen in Japan. Their complex
skills, perfected in the 10th Century, earned them great respect from emperors and
warriors. Fashioning a blade had elements of a religious ceremony, in the course of which
the smith donned special robes and shunned the outside world. Some of the ritual is still
practised, such as hanging a Shinto straw rope above the forge to repel malevolent spirits.

Filled in with red lacquer, this design of a dragon coiled round a blade is copied from one of the many superbly worked swords of the early 17th Century.

A doll's hairline is painted on with sumi, a calligraphic ink mixed from a small flat ink-brick (left).

Oyster-Shell Dolls

Exquisitely dressed dolls have been created painstakingly for more than 300 years, not only as playthings but as works of art. Styles have proliferated over the centuries, some strictly traditional, others reflecting contemporary taste. Those shown here, although not the most conservative, are still produced by time-honoured techniques —even to the mixing of a special finishing-plaster of powdered oyster shells and glue.

From a basic sawdust-and-starch shape (front left) to the demure perfection of the finished heads, the dolls' features develop through successive stages.

8

Pleasures After Dark

An American visitor to Tokyo recently observed with astonishment that the Japanese appeared to be Protestant by day and Mediterranean by night; that in their attitudes towards purity and pleasure, industry and leisure, they had somehow contrived to combine seemingly incompatible extremes. This is strictly a Western view of Tokyo life—and a misleading one. The Japanese themselves have never drawn rigid distinctions between matters pertaining to spirit, body and soul, between absolute good and absolute evil, and so their approach to the entire world of pleasure is strikingly different from that in the West. When it comes to moral values, everything is relative. Indulgence in food, drink and sex may be reprehensible in one context and acceptable in another. Time, place, occasion, age, social position—basically all these things determine what is proper or improper in conduct and behaviour.

It is important to remember this when confronting for the first time the gigantic pleasure pavilion that is modern Tokyo. At night the city is perhaps the most bedazzling in the world. It dazzles with its unparalleled riot of neon lights flashing out mysterious ideographic messages in all colours of the rainbow. It dazzles with the richness and variety of its entertainment—theatres, cinemas, dance halls, floodlit golf ranges, ten-pin bowling alleys, *pachinko* and mah-jong parlours in their thousands. It dazzles with its extraordinary proliferation of restaurants, coffee shops, cabarets, night clubs, homosexual bars, strip-joints and *Toruko-buro* (turkish baths). But it partly dazzles to deceive.

For all its bewildering array of after-dark pleasure pursuits, Tokyo is not the most outrageous fun-city since Sodom and Gomorrah; and for all the garish façade and obvious sensual delights of their capital city, the Japanese are by no means a wildly permissive people. Indeed, in some respects they remain downright Victorian. As Ruth Benedict observes in her classic, supremely penetrating book, "The Chrysanthemum and the Sword", the Japanese can only be described in the most fantastic series of "but also's" that have ever been used for any nation of the world. Contradictions, real or imagined, present themselves at every turn; nothing is quite so black or white as it may seem. And this applies especially to the Japanese in their attitudes towards organized pleasure.

Contrary to expectation, most of Tokyo's night-life closes down before midnight. Prostitution is illegal. Mixed nude bathing is frowned upon and 40 years ago even public dancing was illegal. In reality—although the sight of crowded amusement districts makes it seem otherwise—the average

Glowing, flashing and bustling, the Ginza is a magnet to tourists and big-spending Japanese businessmen with generous expense accounts. Many of the city's more discerning residents favour other entertainment districts offering more subtle pleasures.

Tokyo citizen is not an insatiable hedonist, but a thrifty, industrious individual who likes to get home by 6 p.m., and retire to bed early. But also it is the custom for many—men, at least—to combine business with pleasure, and this partly explains the large numbers who go to restaurants in the evening or linger after work in bars or mah-jong parlours. They may seem to be happily "at play", but as likely as not they are entertaining a client— and taking care he has a good time. Furthermore, many Tokyoites, especially young people, live in such confined spaces that they simply want somewhere to relax in reasonable comfort and style, and this need is particularly well met by the myriad *kissaten* coffee shops where they can find a corner in which to sit and listen to music all evening for the price of a drink.

Of course, by Western standards, Tokyo is undeniably a "swinging city" of the very front rank—a playboy's pleasure-ground offering the best and worst of everything, and equipped to provide for all tastes, however pure or debased. To the foreigner, the most familiar entertainment district is the Ginza, the king of Tokyo's shopping and amusement centres, where whole blocks are crammed with bars and cabarets, each with its own neon sign. Further out, Shinjuku has steadily grown since the 1923 earthquake to rival the Ginza: this district is particularly popular with students and trendy young people in general. But for a complete picture of the Japanese enjoying their leisure hours one cannot do better than visit Asakusa, the oldest and most traditional of Tokyo's entertainment districts.

Asakusa must not be confused with Akasaka, the elegant district described in the previous chapter. Asakusa (Weeds and Shallows) is definitely "lowtown" *shitamachi*, the world of merchants and artisans and commoners, of popular pleasures appealing to the *Edokko*, the Cockney of Tokyo. As long ago as 1899, Basil Hall Chamberlain described Asakusa as a great holiday resort of the middle and lower classes where "nothing is more striking than the juxtaposition of piety and pleasure, of gorgeous altars and grotesque *ex-votos*, of dainty costumes and dingy idols". It is a description, some minor details apart, that still holds good today. In this area, with its noisy crowds and raucous music, its quaint inns and gaudy beer-halls, its impostors, monks, poets, artisans and harlots, its strip-joints and shrines, its festivals and markets, its ugliness and sanctity, much of the rustic bawdiness of old Edo survives.

In the early 6th Century, Asakusa was a small island in the midst of swamps and inlets open to the sea; a place best known for the edible seaweed found in its shallow waters. Then, so legend has it, a miraculous discovery brought fame to the area. One fine March morning in A.D. 628, a nobleman went fishing with his two young retainers near the mouth of the Sumida River. Suddenly the boys cried out with wonder and surprise; their net had come up with a small golden statue of Kannon, the Bodhisattva of mercy. The nobleman respectfully enshrined the image in a simple hut, and families of fishermen and farmers came to worship there in ever-

Undistracted by a barefoot shoeblack napping on the pavement, a pleasure-seeker ponders the attractions of cinema posters on a Ginza wall. The Japanese film industry, renowned abroad for the beauty of its historical and artistic work, also produces many sex-and-violence films, for which there is a substantial audience of young people.

increasing numbers. By 645, that hut had become hopelessly inadequate and it was replaced by the first Sensoji Temple. Subsequently, the temple was destroyed again and again by fire or earthquake, but each time it was built larger or better than before. The greatest building—an imposing structure of wooden pillars and beams all lacquered in red—survived for nearly 300 years until the incendiary raids of 1945. Today, the temple is made of reinforced concrete, but it retains in full the traditional design.

Whatever the truth behind the legend of the fishermen, there is no doubt that the Sensoji Temple was responsible for Asakusa becoming the bawdiest amusement centre of Edo/Tokyo. Reports that the statue had miraculous powers spread through eastern Japan, and in the wake of pilgrims came a great flood of shopkeepers, innkeepers, musicians, fortune-tellers, acrobats, jugglers, beggars and prostitutes. When Ieyasu visited the Sensoji Temple, he found it in a deplorable state, operated by wealthy "monks" who had large families and many concubines. He had the temple rigidly reformed and officially recognized as a major sanctuary. But the character of Asakusa never changed; it has always been as popular for its earthy attractions as for its spiritual consolations.

A customer at a Tokyo streetside snack bar enjoys his privacy—from the shoulders up. Almost all Japanese eating places, including even pavement stalls like this one, have curtains that shield diners from the stares of the idly curious.

During the early Tokugawa days, Japanese society was organized by government decrees down to the minutest details. Prostitution was not only licensed, but regulated with almost pedantic precision, and the most notorious "red light" district of all was officially developed among the paddyfields to the north of Asakusa. More a town than a district, this area is known as Yoshiwara (Happy Fields). Here more than 2,000 high-class courtesans and cheap prostitutes sold their services to lords, merchants, errant monks and samurai, artists and the rest.

The Yoshiwara was but part of an amusement area of far wider scope, a scattered playground centred in Asakusa and full of the atmosphere of *ukiyo* (the floating world). Originally, *ukiyo* was a Buddhist expression that likened human destiny, with its constant uncertainties, to an object floating on stormy waves. In the 17th Century it came to signify a life of pleasure accepted without thought to the future. A Japanese author of the time defined *ukiyo* as a world in which one lives for the moment, gazing at the moon, snow, blossoms and autumn leaves, enjoying *sake*, women and song, and generally drifting with the current of life like a gourd floating downstream. Later, during and after the Genroku era (1688-1704) the expression lost most of its pristine and melancholic shades; more simply it suggested the sweetness and folly of life enjoyed to the hilt.

Since Yoshiwara was part of this floating world, it cannot be strictly labelled a red light district. For it was also a centre of refinement, culture, fashion and wit. Many poets, artists, musicians and writers drew inspiration from its dramatic and colourful atmosphere, and their works attest to its influence on them.

Thirty times over the centuries the Yoshiwara was partly or totally destroyed by natural disasters. In the 1923 earthquake, 600 of its prostitutes lost their lives (the quarter suspended business for one day of memorial services!). Each time, however, this complex of brothels was speedily rebuilt (there was a long period when politicians and other influential citizens had a financial interest in the place); and it enjoyed its greatest boom after the Second World War, until there came such an outcry from the U.S. about the corruption of young G.I.s that General MacArthur was compelled to have it closed down, turning an estimated 40,000 girls out of the brothels and on to the streets. The closure was only temporary, however, and the districts were soon again in full swing.

In the end, it was the protesting women of Japan, not of America, who were largely responsible for the end of the Yoshiwara. Having won the vote in 1945, they put immense pressure on the politicians, and in mid-1957, after many frustrated attempts, they at last saw the passage of anti-prostitution legislation. That law deeply modified habits of relaxation and amusement in Japan; but fundamental attitudes do not change easily, and the spirit of the floating world of Edo still lives on in Asakusa and other entertainment districts.

I last visited Asakusa on New Year's Eve. My taxi dropped me off at the end of Nakamise, the 170-yard approach to the Sensoji Temple.

It was another of those wintry nights when Siberian air sweeps down on Tokyo. The wind had blown away the last webs of city smoke and smog; the sky was deep black, studded brilliantly with stars. Yet, in spite of the cold, there were such throngs of people that the streets somehow felt warm. Everyone was dressed up for the great occasion—women in kimonos of spectacular colours and designs, girls wearing their hair piled up high in the charming traditional style; and a large number of men had donned elegant dark blue kimonos. I walked down Nakamise, a wide alley flanked by souvenir shops, and was drawn into one shop by a hanging scroll that bore an unusually menacing image of Fudo, a fiery god. As I was examining the scroll I heard a familiar voice coming from the back of the shop. I turned and recognized a face from my distant past: Tomiko, a young woman whom I had first met years ago when I was preparing a film of the *ama* fisher-girls who used to dive for abalone off the Boso peninsula. She had been a robust, sunburnt figure then, almost completely naked, and had gone on to become a striptease artist. Now she appeared rather over-dressed, with a white apron protecting her kimono and her hair made up into a shiny, black-lacquered castle with combs and silk flowers.

"Tomiko!" I exclaimed. "What are you doing here?" She smiled enig-matically, and for a moment I felt like saying: "Tomiko, you're as charming as ever—and are you as disreputable as ever?" Fortunately, something told me to be discreet. Perhaps it was all those Buddhas and Bodhisattvas staring at me from the walls of the shop. "My husband has just gone out," Tomiko explained. "He'll be back in a moment. Meanwhile, please do sit down. Welcome! And a Happy New Year! My two sons are away skiing over the holidays. You just cannot keep boys at home any more these days." In a few lines she had judiciously told me of all major developments in her life since last we had met.

Tomiko cleared the inner part of the shop, bade me sit down on a *zabuton* cushion and offered me tea. Then she brought out *o-toso*, the spicy *saké* brewed for the New Year. As we talked about such mundane matters as her children's education and inflation, I could not help reflecting how very appropriate it was that Tomiko should have found such solidly-based respectability in the heart of naughty old Asakusa.

I remembered that when we first met I had asked her how she made a living in the winter. "It used to be awful," she had said, "too cold for any diving. But now I go up to Tokyo and do stripping for a change. I've always gone about naked, so what's the fuss? They actually pay you to take off your clothes." I once went to see Tomiko perform. She seemed happy enough in her work, but I found it all rather sad. I conclude there is a difference between being naked and being undressed; I preferred Tomiko as the unselfconscious nudist who lived more in the water than out of it.

A supplier of plastic "meals", which Tokyo restaurants use to show their dishes, laughs over a novelty (top), an eye-stopping plate of spaghetti. A fuller display of his merchandise (bottom) includes pasta, chops, eggs and chips —evidence of the inroads Western foods have made on the city's eating habits.

But then Tomiko's lost innocence concurs very much with a general trend in Japan. Before the war, I remember, mixed nude bathing was the rule at all *onsen* (hot springs), and it was unremarkable to see men going naked and women bare-breasted when they bathed in rivers, lakes or the sea. Now prudery has taken hold of the country, especially among the young, and mixed bathing is forbidden at most hot springs. Inevitably, of course, such prudery has been accompanied by greater interest in the naked figure as a sex object. The seed of forbidden fruit has taken firm root —hence the proliferation of erotic magazines and *sutorippu* (strip) shows.

The change can be attributed to Western influence (in the same way, kissing is now accepted whereas before the war it was considered a disgusting foreign habit). But more precisely the change can be seen as the outcome of fundamental Japanese traits: the immense national pride and fear of being judged more backward or less sensitive and civilized than other people. This has led the Japanese to imitate the West in many things, both good and bad. It does not, however, mean that they have followed blindly. Basically, they have retained their traditional relaxed attitudes towards sensual pleasure, but as a result of compromise with so many ways of the West they have made those attitudes all the more difficult for the foreigner to comprehend.

For example: changing sexual *mores* have created a psychological mess in many countries, but nowhere is the mess more confusing than in Tokyo, where sex is regulated by rather Victorian attitudes on one side and exploited on the other. Thus we find that Tokyo's amusement districts have hundreds of turkish baths where customers can obtain the most intimate manipulation from highly trained masseuses; and yet straightforward prostitution remains illegal. Then again, nude photographs in imported magazines are subject to official censorship while revolting scenes of sexual violence are quite legal and can be seen in many SM (sado-masochistic) magazines that enjoy wide circulations.

To understand such apparent contradictions, one needs to examine them within the context of old religions and cultural traditions—not to mention superstitions. In the present attitude towards censorship, for example, one detects a distant echo of the ancient view that nudity in everyday life is healthy but in art, unseemly. Even in the powerfully imaginative erotic works of the Tokugawa period, sexual partners were heavily clothed in kimono or *yukata* gowns, or covered by *futon* quilts. At the same time erotic works of didactic value survived (a fine picture scroll depicting sexual positions was recognized as a serious and appropriate item to be included among wedding gifts). Moreover, erotic prints and pictures were esteemed for their power in warding off evil spirits, and it was custom that pornographic books were stored in boxes holding firearms and suits of armour, as a magical protection against fire. Most of the great Japanese artists tried their hand at this genre, but recent waves of puritan

Ignoring the singer and neighbouring revellers, a customer and girl embrace in one of the Ginza's high-priced cabarets. Besides entertaining clients at lunch time, Japanese businessmen customarily take contacts to Tokyo's nightclubs, where female companionship is provided for the evening.

enthusiasm have caused many of these ancient treasures to disappear. One of the greatest libraries of Japanese erotica now sleeps in the secret holds of a collector's storehouse in Tokyo, banned from public view.

Pleasantly warmed with *o-toso saké*, I left Tomiko's souvenir shop to join the great tide of humanity sweeping down towards the Sensoji Temple. The first of 108 tolls was being sounded by the great bronze bell on the near-by hill of Benten, and in front of the temple hundreds of people were pressing around the monumental bronze incense burner. Waves of scented smoke curled into the air—sometimes obscuring faces, sometimes revealing them with dramatic effect—and everywhere people stretched out arms or turned necks or backs towards the fire, in the hope of catching rays of heat reputed to cure all manner of aches and pains.

Here was a scene of profound spiritual feeling and devotion, as evinced by the crowds of pilgrims who climbed the short flight of stairs leading into the temple's main hall and then bowed their heads and joined their hands in silent prayer. Yet, within a few minutes of passing the temple, I was sharply reminded that I was in the heart of one of the most gaudy and bawdy amusement districts in Tokyo. The crowded alleys were flanked by ugly buildings plastered with ideographic advertisements of all sizes, styles and colours, proclaiming the presence of restaurants, bars, coffee-shops, dozens of cheap cinemas and theatres, strip-joints, nude shows and turkish baths. Naked women in voluptuous poses looked down upon me from gigantic placards. Across the torso of one generously endowed female was a large sign: "*Onna Chikan!*" (Female Sex Maniac!). Ostensibly, this neon-lit, concrete jungle was a far cry from the Asakusa of old Edo, the village of thatched-roof huts where harlots and entertainers, innkeepers and *yu-na* (public bath girls) consoled pilgrims worn out by long marches and mystic raptures. But in essence the district has not changed so very much: it is still a traditional mecca for provincial tourists, country bumpkins, and penniless *Edokko*, still a source of both spiritual and sensual refreshment.

I walked in the cold for a while and then entered a small *tendon* (fried fish and rice) shop. I slumped down on a *zabuton* cushion. Tomiko's *o-tose saké* had been stronger than I realized and I felt its effects. Asakusa has won the day, I thought to myself.

While I waited for my New Year breakfast of *zoni*. I pondered the importance of Asakusa to Japanese culture. It was in this *shitamachi* region that the *chonin*, the common people, began to break out of the cultural straitjacket imposed by the ruling classes. From the late 17th Century onwards, samurai no longer set the fashion, were no longer aped by admiring commoners. Indeed, the reverse became true as the *chonin* rejected academic literature, art and drama and looked for a mirror of their own lives—their own pleasures, tragedies and comedies. It led to new forms of expression, more free and realistic and spontaneous; to a people's culture.

In seeking realism and spontaneity, the *chonin* might easily have rushed towards extreme vulgarity; but happily the legacy of Buddhism's idealistic philosophy tempered this quest. *Chonin* culture shed new light on human situations while maintaining superb imaginative freedom; it distorted and reassembled the world of appearances as it pleased in its search for inner sparks of truth. In the world of drama, the people's reaction against entertainments designed for the aristocracy found its most exciting and colourful expression in the development of *Kabuki*, an entirely new form of theatre that combined traditional and popular Japanese culture: a spectacular *pot pourri* that embraced both high tragedy and low comedy, and blended elements of dance, mime, acrobatics and music. For the ordinary townsfolk of Edo, starved of excitement and lavish display, it offered a glorious escape into a world where they could feast their eyes on resplendent costumes and settings, and also delight in stories that actually had clever commoners outwitting their social superiors, sometimes even winning battles against samurai bullies. The form had far greater zest and relevance, naughtiness and earthiness, than either *Bunraku* (puppet-theatre) or the classical *Noh*; and it enjoyed the kind of mass impact and appeal that the Elizabethan playhouse achieved in Shakespeare's day.

Kabuki was founded in 1603 by a woman—a dancing girl called O-Kuni, whose act combined ritual dance and erotic by-play—and originally it was performed exclusively by women. Over the years, however, performances tended more and more towards obscenity, and in 1629 women were banned forever from participating. Young men took over the roles with equally unfortunate results: sodomy became a theme for humourous treatment and samurai began fighting over boy-actors. As a result, Kabuki was banned in 1651 for two years. On revival it could be performed legally only by mature men—a requirement that produced a class of female impersonators still very much alive today.

A Kabuki performance lasts about five to six hours, with a long break in between. The atmosphere in the theatre is essentially *laissez-faire*, and it is perfectly proper for members of the audience to cat-nap during a show or take a break when they please. At its best, it is a tremendously dramatic and thrilling spectacle, one that still flourishes in Tokyo, being played with distinction at the Kabukiza Theatre bordering on the Ginza. While it developed as the theatre of the masses, it cannot be said to have quite the same hold on people today. Nevertheless, *Kabuki* is very much a permanent pillar of the Japanese culture and, most importantly it is one form of traditional Japanese entertainment that has gone unchanged for more than a century. Rather sadly, the same cannot be said of some of Tokyo's other age-old pleasure pursuits, as I was to discover on another winter evening when, in the company of two old friends, one an Italian, the other a Japanese, I visited a large Tokyo night club.

Street musicians seek to lure customers to a new restaurant that has been decorated with artificial flowers for the occasion. Called chindonya, they will move along the streets striking their drums and cymbals in succession.

Miyu, short for Miyume (Beautiful dream) rested her head on my shoulder and said in a raucous voice: "Neh, Mr. Guest, will you buy me a whisky? *On ze rokksu*, please. Oh, I am so thirsty!" She was about 25 years old, dressed in a low-cut green gown that revealed just enough soft flesh to make one wish for more; and she had small, delicate hands that one could picture cradling a lotus flower. But there was something hard and ruthless in her eyes and around the mouth, and every time she opened the latter she destroyed any illusion of virginal beauty by flashing too many gold teeth. "Neh, Mr. Guest," she went on, "buy me a dish of fried prawns. Come on now, don't be such a miser."

For half an hour this Tokyo night club hostess had chattered about her favourite cars and perfumes. Now we had exhausted these subjects and it seemed that nothing else interested her except matters pertaining to food and drink. All around us, on circular sofas set in cosy corners, other girls were similarly engaged in light conversation with a variety of customers, mostly Japanese. There must have been several hundred of them, some in Western dress, some in kimonos, nearly all of them elegant, superficially attractive and young. There were also many teenage boys with delicate, white, androgynous faces serving as waiters. Tough-looking men with sinister eyes, uniformly dinner-jacketed and moving silently about the carpeted floor, escorted customers in and out, and supervised proceedings.

It has often been said that Tokyo needs few psychiatrists because it has so many hostesses, and viewing this kind of scene one begins to appreciate how the sofa in night club or bar may well act as a substitute for the analyst's couch. Here, in a world strictly not for wives, the Japanese businessman unwinds and recharges his batteries by way of an evening of carefree conversation and ego-boosting female companionship. And it is a measure of the therapeutic value of such diversion that the employee's *kaisha* company more often than not foots the bill.

Traditionally, the geisha (cultivated person) fulfilled this soothing function. But the geisha is sadly on the wane in Japan; her services are far too costly, too esoteric and exquisite for our rough materialistic times. Moreover, such a delicate flower of supreme refinement—the end-product of years of painstaking education and training—could never be cultivated in sufficient numbers to meet the demand in an overcrowded metropolis such as Tokyo. Millions of Japanese men would dearly like to escape the frenetic hustle and bustle of city life and briefly enter the cultured oasis of a genuine geisha house. But that is essentially a rich man's luxury now, far beyond the pocket of the average Tokyoite. Quality has been totally sacrificed for quantity; and to serve the *hoi polloi*, tens of thousands of hostesses have taken over. Tokyo is reckoned to have 80,000 hostesses. In no way are they to be confused with that rare orchid, the geisha. Virtually any girl can become a hostess, irrespective of looks, charms or social status. She may be a crypto-prostitute or a genuine virgin, even have a husband and children. Some are charming, some witty and intelligent, some read books and appreciate good music.

"Beautiful dream" again rested her head on my shoulder, again flashed her gold teeth. "Neh, Mr. Guest," she sighed, "the prawns were good, so good, but how can I digest them without another whisky *on ze rokksu*?" It was time to be leaving. We had only come to this Tokyo night club because one of my friends had hoped to meet a superior hostess, called Yoshiko, whom he particularly liked. But Yoshiko no longer worked at the club, and so we were just three more casual customers, sitting prey to vultures masquerading as delicate butterflies.

We took our leave, piled into a taxi, and crossed half the city in search of more animated night-life. It was midnight now, and that really is the middle of the night in Tokyo—the streets wide and empty, the city largely a no-man's land of stray cats and lonely policemen patrolling their beat. Some establishments serving food as well as drink remained open. But most bars were closed and the dance halls had long since played their last waltz or rock number.

Suddenly we began to see people again—lights, traffic, crowds of *sake*-warmed revellers. "Ah, here we are in Shinjuku," said Carlo gaily, as though welcoming an old friend. Shinjuku, once a frontier town of Edo, is now the real Fuyajo ("Nightless City") of Tokyo, a 20th-Century Asakusa, where pilgrims gather not to worship a diminutive golden Bodhisattva fished out of the sea 15 centuries ago, but to get inebriated with illusions, to pray for sensations, to chase the fleeting pleasures of the floating world.

It is a sprawling district of coffee shops and parlours for *pachinko* players endlessly flipping ball-bearings into metal cups marked "win" or "lose". The only sure winners here in the very late hours are the *yakuza* gangsters ever busy with their protection rackets and various illegal spin-offs. They are to be seen lurking in corners everywhere.

Finally, after Carlo had dragged us around more drinking dens than I care to remember, we had our last *sake* and headed for home. As we drove off by taxi, my eyes wandered up to the tops of a cluster of new skyscrapers rising majestically above the warrens and disorderly shacks. Fifty storeys up in the sky there was definitely a premonition of dawn.

Were those towers, I wondered, a vision of the Tokyo of tomorrow? Perhaps. Paradoxically, history shows Tokyo to be the most vulnerable and the most resilient of all the great cities of the world. The gods may periodically unleash their earthquakes, fires and floods. New hazards of massive pollution and congestion may become an ever-escalating menace. Nonetheless, architects, planners and sociologists believe that this city is destined to grow upwards and outwards, that by the year 2000, it could extend from Chiba to Kobe (more than 300 miles)—a megalopolis of some 60 million inhabitants. What an awesome thought! What a commentary of the extraordinary industry and indomitable spirit of a people.

A Portfolio of Urban Patterns

The rice-straw wrappings on these two-foot-high saké casks—piled up as offerings at a shrine—combine their calligraphic legends into a tapestried design.

To understand a city it is necessary to penetrate to the truth behind the appearance, especially a city as puzzling and contradictory as Tokyo. But to achieve true familiarity with a place, it is also important to reverse the process for a while—to forget the duty of trying to understand or interpret, and float effortlessly on the surface, enjoying whatever texture the eye may happen to rest on. In Tokyo, the rewards of such a sensory sampling are rich and subtle. The instinctive feeling of the Japanese for decorative detail seems to ensure that, even amid the turmoil and chaos of the modern megalopolis, there is always something harmonious to look at. Ordinary objects compose themselves almost of their own accord into patterns and patchworks, so that a rack of wooden seals, a pile of temple gifts—even a crowd—becomes part of Tokyo's mosaic.

Hand-made wooden name stamps, less than half an inch across, are offered for sale nestling in a matrix of labelled pigeonholes. Until quite recently they were an essential part of life in Tokyo, since no signature was legally complete without their imprint. The large range available covers all common names, and other stamps can be quickly carved when they are required.

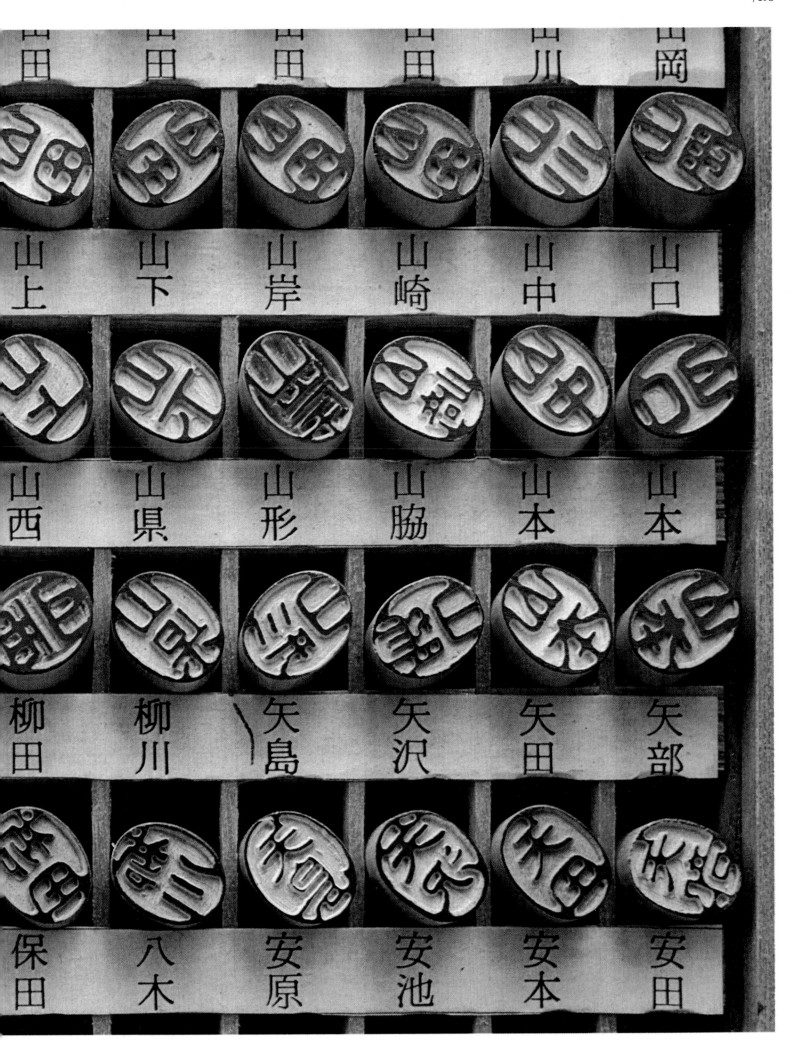

山田　山田　山田　山田　山川　山岡

山上　山下　山岸　山崎　山中　山口

山西　山県　山形　山脇　山本　山本

柳田　柳川　矢島　矢沢　矢田　矢部

保田　八木　安原　安池　安本　安田

White paper strips, clustered like little birds, are printed horoscopes that are sold at shrines and temples. Once read, they are customarily left tied to something holy: temple door handles or twigs in the temple garden. These have roosted in a wire fence at the Asakusa Kannon Temple near Ueno Park.

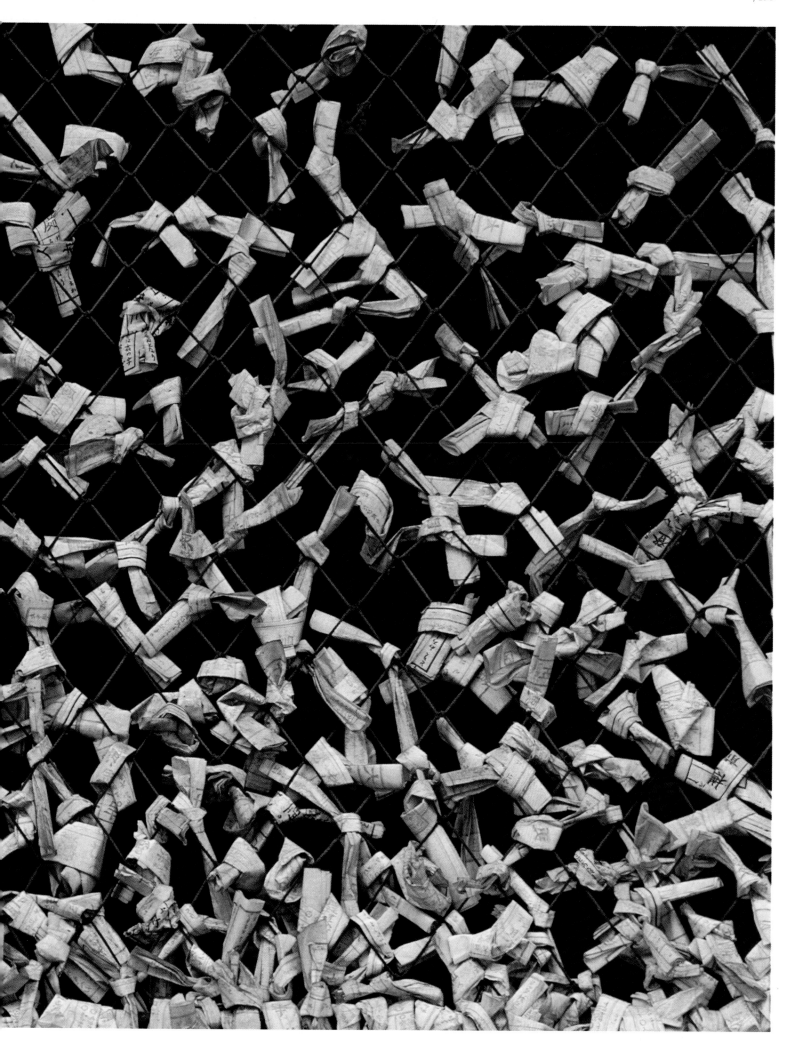

Conical hats worn by the supporters of one team at a university baseball match dapple the stands with dabs of red. The hats double ingeniously as megaphones.

Bibliography

Agency for Cultural Affairs, *Japanese Religion.* Kodansha International Ltd., Japan, 1972.

Akamatsu, Paul, *Meiji 1868, Revolution and Counter-Revolution in Japan.* George Allen and Unwin Ltd., London, 1972.

Alcock, Sir Rutherford, *The Capital of the Tycoon* (2 vols.). Longman, Green, Longman, Roberts, and Green, London, 1863.

Benedict, Ruth, *The Chrysanthemum and the Sword.* Routledge & Kegan Paul, London, 1946.

Black, John, *Young Japan* (2 vols.). Oxford University Press, 1968.

Busch, Noel F., *Two Minutes to Noon.* Simon and Schuster, New York, 1962.

Caiger, G., *Tell Me About Tokyo.* Hokuseido, Tokyo, 1939.

Chamberlain, Basil Hall, *Japanese Things.* Charles E. Tuttle & Co., Tokyo, 1971.

Condon, Camy and Nagasawa, K., *Kites, Crackers and Craftsmen.* Shufunotomo, Tokyo, 1973.

De Becker, J. E., *The Nightless City.* Charles E. Tuttle & Co., New York, 1971.

Hawks, Francis L., *Narrative of the Expedition of an American Squadron to the China Seas and Japan.* Macdonald, London, 1954.

Hibbett, Howard, *The Fighting World in Japanese Fiction.* Oxford University Press, 1959.

Japan National Tourist Organization, *The New Official Guide, Japan.* Japan Travel Bureau, Inc., Japan, 1975.

Kaempfer, Engelbert, *The History of Japan.* AMS Press, New York, 1971.

Kirkup, James, *Heaven, Hell and Hara-Kiri.* Angus and Robertson, London, 1974.

Kirkup, James, *Tokyo.* Phoenix House, London, 1966.

Lee, Frank, *A Tokyo Calendar.* Hokuseido, Tokyo, 1934.

Leonard, Jonathan Norton, *Early Japan.* Time-Life Books, Amsterdam, 1976.

Maraini, Fosco, *Meeting with Japan.* Hutchinson and Co., London, 1959.

Mogi, Hitoshi, *A Historical Study of the Development of Edo 1600-1860.* Tokyo, 1966.

Morris, John, *Traveller from Tokyo.* New York, 1943.

Nouët, Noël, *Histoire de Tokyo.* Presses Universitaires de France, Paris, 1961.

Piggot, Juliet, *Japanese Mythology.* Paul Hamlyn, London, 1969.

Pezeu-Massabuau, J., *L'Agglomération de Tokyo.* La Documentation Française, Paris, 1974.

Rudofsky, Bernard, *The Kimono Mind.* Victor Gollancz, London, 1966.

Sadler, A. L., *The Maker of Modern Japan, Tokugawa Ieyasu (1542-1616).* Norton, New York, 1941.

Sansom, George B., *History of Japan* (3 vols.). Stanford University Press, 1958-1963.

Sansom, Katherine, *Living in Tokyo.* New York, 1937.

Satow, Ernest, *A Diplomat in Japan.* Oxford University Press, 1968.

Scott Morton, W., *The Japanese, How They Live and Work.* David and Charles, Newton Abbot, 1973

Smith, Bradley, *Japan—A History in Art.* The Hamlyn Publishing Group, 1972.

Von Siebold, P. F., Dr., *Manners and Customs of the Japanese in the Nineteenth Century.* Charles E. Tuttle & Co., New York, 1973.

Yazaki, Takeo, *The Japanese City.* Rutland: Japan Publications Trading Co., Tokyo, 1963.

Yazaki, Takeo, *The Socioeconomic Structure of the Tokyo Metropolitan Complex.* University of Hawaii, 1970.

Acknowledgements

The editors wish to thank the following: Jay Brennan, Tokyo; Charles Dettmer, Thames Ditton, Surrey; Jill Gribbin, Brighton, Sussex; Neil Hepburn, London; Shoichi Imai, Tokyo; Japanese Information Centre, London; Eri Matsubara, Tokyo; Takeshi Murumatsu, Tokyo; Lucille Napear, Tokyo; S. Parker, London; B. W. Robinson, London; G. G. Smith, Crawley, Sussex; Nakanori Tashiro, Tokyo; Bill Tingey, London; John K. Wheeler, Tokyo.

Index

Numerals in italics indicate a photograph
or drawing of the subject mentioned.

Colour reproduction by Irwin Photography Ltd., at their Leeds PDI Scanner Studio.
Filmsetting by C. E. Dawkins (Typesetters) Ltd., London, SE1 1UN.
Printed and bound in Italy by Arnoldo Mondadori, Verona.